i

Been Around

Been Around

Memoirs of a

Brown County Troubadour

By Robbie Bowden

(as told to Jeff Tryon)

Published by Jetpub2020, P.O. Box 1962, Nashville, Indiana 47448

ISBN: 9798670936019

Jetpub 2020

A Jetpub publication
P.O. Box 1962
Nashville, IN 47448
Jetpub2020@gmail.com

Dedications:

To Karen:

"My Forever Brand New Friend"

To Dave:

Brother in spirit and song

To Nancy June:

Dear heart

To Deb:

Lyricist, author, poet, friend

To Erin:

Songbird daughter

To Stephanie:

My sister angel

To Jeff:

An articulate wordsmith

Foreword (into the past!)
By Dave Gore

Most of the people who live in Brown County, Indiana these days are transplants, moved here from the big cities to enjoy the scenic beauty and the laid-back lifestyle. Few have come for the economic possibilities, unless they've moved here to try and make a buck off of the tourist trade.

Very seldom do you run into a true native, someone who was either born here or has deep family roots planted in Brown County.

Although he was born in Seattle, Washington and brought here at only a few months of age, Robbie Bowden is about as close to a true Brown County native as you'll get these days. His family settled here in the early 1800's. He's considered Brown County home all his life, though he's travelled to many states plying and honing his skills as a singer/songwriter and musician, as most have had to do to "make it" in the music business.

My family didn't immigrate to Brown County until 1951. My grandparents bought 100 acres north of Nashville in the late 1940's, and convinced my parents to come visit this beautiful part of America.

They fell in love with it and decided to give it a shot. My brother Steve and I are still here, and although we're not "natives", we're "locals", a term I'm convinced you have to earn by being a part of and contributing to the community.

I met Robbie Bowden in the late 1950's. Boy Scout Troop 90 had been formed and we met on a hike to an area in Brown County State Park called "Little Blue". We discovered a mutual love of Mad Magazine and have shared that zany sense of humor to this day. I can remember hanging out at the Bowden home many times listening to comedy albums by the likes of Jonathan Winters, Tom Lehrer and Stan Freeburg.

Rob's family had the first color TV, before many families I knew. It was low-def by today's standards with kind of a strange green color, but hey, it was better than black and white. I always felt like part of the family there with Robbie, his younger brother Rick, and little sister Laura.

The seeds of Robbie's love of music sprouted early in that little house on Washington Street as his father, Bob, was an avid music lover and singer himself.

During the 1960's Robbie was in the high school band, then he and I and three girls formed a folk quintet, having been influenced by the popular folk movement.

He moved on to rock and roll during the British Invasion led by the Beatles and other bands, including American ones.

Rob and I have enjoyed almost 60 years of singing and making music together. Although I consider him much more musically advanced than myself, he has always been patient with my technical shortcomings and always glad to share a new way to form a chord or play a rhythm part. We have always shared a natural ability to vocally harmonize.

I must also note here that Rob is a veritable warehouse of historical musical trivia, able to retrieve the name of some obscure artist or song long-forgotten by most. And not just rock or country, but he's a long-time successful player of radio station

WFIU's "Ether Game" which quizzes listeners on classical music trivia. (He's "First Bass")

Robbie and I are lifelong musical brothers and we've shared a ton of laughs over the years.

A troubadour, "road scholar", and local music legend; I'm glad he came back home to Brown County to continue his musical legacy.

"And now... Forward! Into the Past!"

Dave Gore, Summer 2020

Spirits of Home

It was Labor Day weekend, 2011, ninety degrees and headed for a hundred. Steamy and sticky, we were sent back to the 1920's on the front porch of the Vene Shrock house on Jefferson Street.

Old friends gathered to fill the idle time. The spirit of the rustic souls who lived here before came alive in us.

So we spun the stories and jokes and memories. Somehow those moments set our hearts at ease and we were at home in a part of this lovely place of childhood and past lives.

An opening of a door to another time...

A stranger walked by and heard us laughing and she smiled. She could see we were happy to be where we wanted to be,

where we should be

where we have to be and

like the spirits from before,

where we will always be.

-Robbie Bowden

Part One:

Youthful Exuberance

C. Carey Cloud created this fanciful map of
Brown County, Indiana in 1932.

A Brown County Boy

*"Four years old, and
all was right with the world..."*

I'm a sixth-generation Brown Countian.

My great-grandmother was a Kelley, who came here in the 1830's. My great grandfather came from Somerset, England, in the southwest, down by Bristol and Bath, not too far from Wales. He came here a few years later and they met and married.

So, I'm related to the "Kelley Hill" Kelley's – Eudora Kelly. Rick Kelley told me that he and I are fourth cousins.

I consider myself a Brown Countian, even though I happened to be born in Seattle, because my dad was in the Navy during WWII. I was born in July of 1945. The war was still on in the Pacific.

My mother was from a little town in southwest Minnesota called Kensington. It was famous for the "Kensington Stone", supposedly a Viking stone tablet. I think maybe it turned out to be a scam.

She went out to Seattle to live with her cousin and work in a defense plant. She met my dad, and they got married on New Year's Eve, 1943, and I was born July 7, 1945. Pop was on a hospital ship in the South Pacific somewhere.

As soon as the war was over, which was not more than a couple of months after I was born, we came back here. We lived in Indianapolis for a short time, because my dad had a job up there, but he hated the city. He was a Brown County boy.

My first recollections of Brown County itself are out on McLary Road. Old Mrs. McLary lived in half the house and we lived in the other half, rented it from her. I think it burned down in the 1960's.

I have a really fond memory of that house. I don't know why, but this has stuck with me.

I was four years old. It was in the Fall, Indian Summer weather, shirtsleeve weather. I remember my dad sitting on the porch, smoking his pipe, my brother running around crazy, you know, two years old. My sister Laura hadn't been born yet.

I looked out across this cornfield, with these cornstalks kind of blowing in the breeze; it was this feeling of utter contentment. I've never forgotten that. All was right with the world.

Four years old, and all was right with the world...

Later, when I was in my twenties, my mother told me that when I was three or four years old, I would find a place where I thought I couldn't be heard and sing to myself, thinking that nobody could hear me.

I was probably singing something that I had heard on the radio. My dad always had a radio. There was always music in the house, from the time I can remember when we lived out on McLary Road.

It was 1949, we didn't even have a record player then, just a radio. We listened to popular music of the day, "Hit Parade" of the late 40's and early 50's. Probably people like Joe Stafford and Bing Crosby, Perry Como, Frank Sinatra.

The radio stations we mostly listened to were WIBC out of Indianapolis, and WFBM. Those were probably the two big stations then. WXLW in the late 50's and early 60's, they played a mixture of stuff.

Pop liked big band music and he loved close harmonies. He liked male a cappella choirs like Norman Luboff and Mitch Miller, stuff like that. Pop liked barbershop music, too.

So I heard that from an early age. I think that's where I got my taste for harmonizing. I have a natural ear for it. I can find a harmony pretty easily.

Both of my grandfathers were still alive up until about my sixth year.

My mother got fed up with my dad's drinking and grabbed my brother and I - he was just a toddler - and we went up to Minnesota. We spent six months up there. So I got to be with my grandpa Karl Hegg. Hegg, which is Swedish, was my mother's maiden name.

So I'm Swedish and English.

I remember my grandpa Bowden, James Joshua Bowden, he would come out to our place when we lived out in one of those rental houses across from the fairgrounds (on Old State Road 46).

The landlord at the time was a man named Ansel Powell, who was related to Mark and Von Williamson's family. It was pretty primitive. Cold running water, that was it.

Then we moved into town and we moved into the Hester House, which is on the corner of Mound and Jefferson. I was five. My sister Laura was born in that house, delivered by a county health nurse.

Hester house

Pop was in the high school choir. Somewhere, somehow a music professor from Franklin College heard my father singing and he said, "I can get you on the radio."

There were a lot of live performances by local people on the radio back in those days. But I guess he had what they called in those days "mic fright", nervousness about singing on the radio, and he backed out. He didn't do it.

8

He was even given a second chance, but he couldn't do it.

But he sang in church and occasionally took a solo and he would sing barbershop with his friends Gaither Eads, Bill McGrayel, Bill Gore - Dave's dad, Pods Miller - Steve's dad, and a guy who ran the Nashville State Bank, Eldon Ploetz.

They just got together, probably at the church, I think, and just jammed, for fun.

After the Hester house, we moved into the Vene Shrock house (at the corner of Jefferson and Pittman House Lane). We lived there for four years, from the time I was nine till I was 13.

Vene Shrock house

I mowed grass for the Christian church and clipped the weeds around the walkways.

I had a paper route delivering the Columbus Republican, it was called in those days. (Now The Republic.) I had about 30 customers around town.

I had a bicycle, I think my parents paid five dollars for it. It was a 24-inch girl's bicycle that we got from Rudy Crabtree's sister, Mary Elizabeth. I was probably 10 or 11.

I saved up my money, saved up 30 dollars and my folks chipped in ten dollars, and we went to Martinsville and bought a J.C. Higgins bicycle at the J.C. Penny's store. It was a really nice bike, really strong, well built. I loved it.

Nashville was a much smaller, more primitive town then. There were no street signs, nobody knew what the names of the streets were.

Fifth Grade

There was a bunch of us kids, the Jefferson Street kids. Dave Gore, Kenny Seitz, Buddy Greller, Clyde and Lance McDonald, Pat Riley lived up on Orchard Hill. Mary Kilgore. And my cousins, Uncle Ray Bowden's daughters, Rachel, Connie, Susie, and Barbara and the three sons, Bill, Jack and James. Ray was my dad's oldest brother. I'm still close with those girls.

The Jefferson Street kids.

We rode our bikes everywhere.

I remember this one summer, we turned Nashville into a racecourse, a bicycle racecourse in a figure-eight shape. It covered several blocks. And we had a bicycle race. We'd take so many laps around town. To us kids, it was a marathon.

And I won the race. It's one of my favorite childhood memories.

Of course, we went down to the creek a lot (Salt Creek), and we'd go up Greasy Creek, too, and catch crawdads.

We would go down to "the mouth", we called it, the mouth of Greasy Creek, there was good fishing in that area down there. And then down West of the bridge (over Salt Creek at SR46 and SR135) was an area we called "the bluff".

Salt Creek Bridge, 1930 (Frank Hohenberger)

We had a rope swing hanging off of a Sycamore tree and we would swing out and drop into the creek. There was a nice swimming hole there, underneath that Sycamore tree.

There were these two boys from Manhattan, New York City whose grandmother lived up on Artist's Drive, Tom and

11

Donald McMannus. We met up with those guys one summer, and we did all kinds of things with them while they were here for the summer.

They loved it here.

The McMannus boys and my brother and I rented these canoes from Jack Weddle and we put in at about Greasy Creek and went down to about Yellowwood (Lake/state forest). That was a trip; that was real hoot.

The McMannus boys' grandfather was a man named Willard Patty who had been athletic director at IU. There's an athletic award over there still called the Patty Award.

Grandpa Patty would put on these backyard olympics and we'd do standing broad jumps, sprints, things like that. They had a lot of property.

We also had an Indian club. There were trails all down in the woods below the house where the McMannus boys were staying. And we had a club called "Sons of Manitou'. We'd run around those paths with breachclouts on.

Those city boys just loved it here.

My mother worked at the Colonial Room Restaurant in season, so Pop was in charge of us kids and he used to take us on drives. He loved to go roam the backroads.

When he was growing up, what he did for entertainment when he wasn't involved in school sports or whatever, he walked the backroads and logging trails and whatnot around the county every weekend. He loved the outdoors.

I still love to go down those back roads, reminisce, tell stories about my youth... I've done that with my friend Karen many times.

When I was in the sixth grade, I started taking clarinet lessons from Mr. Brodus, Herman Brodus, who was the band teacher at the time. My dad had played clarinet in the high school band and that's what he wanted me to play as well.

So we went over to a music store in Columbus and bought a Bundy clarinet. A student model made by Selmer. It wasn't wooden like a good clarinet should be, it was some kind of plastic, and I played that all through school up to my senior year, when I bought a wooden Selmer from my cousin, Connie Bowden.

We used to sneak up after dark on the hill at Pods Miller's place and swipe some of his Concorde Grapes. I think he knew we did it. And we would go back behind the old gymnasium, where we would go to smoke, and we'd eat those grapes.

I remember climbing up on top of the gym roof one time just to see what it was like to be up there looking down. It was a thrill, I guess to a 12-year old.

We got caught smoking once, by the Sheriff, Bill Percifield.

Dave Gore is two years younger than me; but his birthday is the day after mine. I'm July 7, Dave is July 8.

Dave's Dad had the Orchard Hill Motel built. And they lived there in a house behind the motel.

I knew Dave along about the time he was 10 or 11 and I was 12 or 13, but I thought he was a brat. He borrowed my bicycle one day, and he bent the handlebars or something and I was upset with him.

But then, we went on a winter hike together.

He had just joined the Boy Scouts. I had been in the Boy Scouts a couple of years, I was 14. And Frank Zody, who was my track coach in high school, he took us on a hike in an area of the state park that was completely undeveloped – just a bunch of pine forest that the CCC's had planted back during the depression. He called it "Little Blue".

And Dave and I got to talking about how we both liked Mad Magazine. And that's where the friendship started, maybe about the winter 1959.

That's also a fond memory of mine, frozen in time. It was just one of those perfect winter days. It was cold, but there was sunshine. We were hiking in the woods, we were young. It was uplifting.

It was spiritual, or as close to a spiritual moment as a 14-year-old can get...

So Dave and I started running around together more and more, especially through school, and we've been the best of friends since school.

When I was around 14, I had a job washing dishes at the Colonial Room Restaurant for Jay and Verna Kilgore. My mom was a part time cook there, that's how I got the gig.

The first time I ever sang in public with other people was probably at church.

I knew that I could carry a tune pretty well. Most of the girls in the Junior High age group, they'd just blast it out. They'd sing as loud as they could. And I could keep up with them, and I did a couple of times, but I got embarrassed. I thought I was being foolish. I didn't know what to think of my singing in public.

They would have a sunrise service on Easter Sunday out at the Lower Shelter house out at the state park. The Methodist Church and the Nashville Christian Church, which was my church when I was a kid, would combine their choirs.

14

And to this day I have several songs that I remember from growing up in the Nashville Christian Church, like "Softly and Tenderly" and "In the Garden" – those are my two favorites. I made a medley of those two songs – first, Jesus is calling you, and then you're in the garden with Him.

Nashville Christian Church, 1952
(Frank Hohenberger)

I belong to the Methodist church now, and I sing the same songs. I find it spiritually uplifting to sing with other people.

At church, I've done some songs with just me and the guitar, and a couple of Christmases ago Carolyn Dutton and I did the song from the first Brown County Christmas album, "A Cradle in Bethlehem". We got a standing ovation from the congregation.

That's a great song. I've had people request it in July.

Nashville Grafitti

"Six songs for a quarter, or a nickel apiece…"

After we lived in the Vene Shrock house, in 1958 my folks bought a house on Washington Street, two houses down from where the new high school would be built.

My dad, who was a house painter by trade, got a Veteran's Administration loan and bought the house on a quarter acre lot. It was blue with white trim and it had a nice yard and a garden plot that had gooseberries. It cost $7,500 - fifty-two bucks a month for 25 years.

I remember when I was out in Arizona, it would have been 1983, I guess, mom called me and said, "I just paid my last payment on the house."

Isn't that great? You don't find things like that any more.

My brother sold it for $65,000 in the early-to-mid-1980's. I imagine the lot would go for that now, at least.

That house burned down a few years ago. It's just an empty lot now. The Nashville General store parks their bus there.

Nashville High School, 1930
(Frank Hohenberger)

I attended the old Nashville High School in the building that used to sit on Van Buren Street roughly where the Artist Colony Inn sits today. While I was in high school, they consolidated all the county high schools into one Brown County High School in Nashville.

I was in the second class to graduate from the new Brown County High School in 1963.

I lettered in cross-country and track. Our track was the rectangular parking lot in front of the school and we ran our cross country meets out at the old nine-hole golf course at the Brown County Country Club. I was also student manager of the basketball team, for which I also received a letter.

I played clarinet in the high school band. I had started on clarinet in sixth grade and played it all through twelfth grade.

When I was a Senior, I was first-chair, so I got to take all the clarinet solos. Had to. I was playing two and three notes above the staff, which I'd never done before.

High school daze...

You know, when I graduated from high school I put that clarinet on the shelf and I never touched it again, although I have been known to play a recorder now and again. The fingering is the same. I've used a recorder in a couple of recording sessions. I eventually traded that clarinet for an electric guitar.

In high school, Dave and I used to go into the "family side" of the Pine Room to listen to country music on the jukebox – Buck Owens and George Jones, guys like that. That's kind of where we got inspired to sing those old country songs a couple of years later.

We'd go into the Pine Room and get a couple of cokes, split an order of fries and listen to those country songs.

We used to hitchhike out to the swimming pool at the state park, then we would sneak in. We would go down below the covered bridge and cross the creek and sneak in and come around to the bathhouse.

Claris Keaton was the superintendent of the park at that time, and he caught us sneaking in one day and he made us go up to the gatehouse and pay. I don't know what it was in those days, the early 1960's, I think a quarter.

Pool at Brown County State Park
(Frank Hohenberger)

In summertime, the park pool was quite the social scene. The old pool was a really interesting structure, not like this Olympic-standard pool they've got now. It had a big round medium depth part. There was a kid's pool and a deep section with two diving boards, three foot and nine foot.

Another hotbed of teenage activity in those days was Jerry's Root Beer Stand (on what is now Old School Way, just south of Main Street). That was one of my haunts. The Brown County Winery shop is there now.

20

We'd walk up after school, put a quarter in the jukebox and you got six songs for a quarter, or a nickel apiece. I'd put on Duane Eddy or Maurice Williams and the Zodiacs, groups like that,

"Stay... just a little bit longer..."

We would sit in the back booth and smoke. And Jerry Canan, who owned the place at the time, would come back there and he would say, "You know, I'm not going to tell you not to smoke back here, but you young people don't need to be smoking cigarettes."

Of course, we ignored him...

(L-R) Dave Gore, Gary Deaver, Robbie Bowden

It was a drive-in in those days, ala "Happy Days" or "American Grafitti". Kids would come from Columbus and Bloomington to hang out at Jerry's Root Beer Stand.

And these souped-up cars would show up. There was a guy from Bloomington, his nickname was "Nockie" and he drove a '46 Chevy with spun aluminum hubcaps and flames on the side. He and Ronnie King would get into an ice cream eating contest to see who could eat the most ice cream, and we would all stand around and watch them. They'd both be about half sick when it was over.

The stretch of straight road (on State Road 46 West) over the hill and down from Town Hill Drive, that was our drag strip. There's a log house on the left and it was lived in by Clayton and Anna George and we called it the "Clayton George memorial drag strip."

Senior photo

We worked trimming Christmas trees a couple of summers.

Carl Carpenter and others had Christmas tree farms. It was a big industry for little Brown County; they shipped clear to Florida.

Von Williamson crew-bossed tree trimming crews for different growers, made up mostly of high school kids or those just out of high school. Dan Reeves, the son of artist and Brown County genealogy buff Kenneth Reeves, worked with me on the first crew I was on for Von.

Billy Jo Kritzer and I were on a crew together. He was in my class, the class of '63, we ran cross country together. In the first class to graduate from the new school were Steve Miller, Bill Robertson, and Rudy Crabtree.

They had a hell of a basketball team. They were 20-3 their senior year.

They had been the reserves and they all got bumped up to varsity; Rudy Crabtree, Steve Miller, Bill Robertson, Joe Petro and James Robert Kennedy, Don Acton, a couple of other guys. Their sixth man was kind of a floater. Then when they were seniors, they had Steve Kritzer at forward and he was wicked. He wasn't that tall but he was big, built like a football player.

When the new State Highway 46 extension came through, (from the north gate State Park entrance to the intersection with State Road 135 at the Salt Creek bridge) it changed the town.

The famous Brown County artists, most of them were still alive when I was in high school. Adolph Shulz, V.J. Cariani, Georges LaChance, and Leota Loop all lived into the 1960's. Marie Goth, Dale Bessire and C. Curry Bohm all lived into the 1970's.

The summer after I graduated…

"I heard you picked up guitar…"

The summer after I graduated from high school, some of my good friends and I started singing together.

I was class of '63, but I ran with '64 and '65 class people. My really close friends were Dave Gore, Anna Lee Wheeler and Jenny Wheeler, and Nancy Stouffer, who in those days I had a big crush on.

In that summer after I graduated, we just came together one day. Nancy, Jenny and Anna and Dave and I, we were sitting at the pump house there on the Village Green, by the old library, singing together, just harmonizing just for fun.

Pods Miller came walking by and he encouraged us, "You guys sound great!" Keep it up!"

So we had an a cappella folk singing group called the "Cherry Hill Singers" because Nancy lived in a place called Cherry Hill. We'd sing Peter, Paul and Mary, Joan Baez, Kingston Trio, that kind of stuff.

We got a couple of gigs, did some pep rallies, homecoming, things like that. We did some things for civic organizations, Lions Club, Kiwanis, for like, five bucks apiece.

After Annalee and Jenny had gone on their way, Dave and Nancy and I sang together. We were just the best of friends, we've been that way since school. We were like the three musketeers. But then she moved to California.

That's where she met Bob Cheevers, a few years later, which is how we met Bob Cheevers, through Nancy.

Dave and I had started singing a cappella in high school, old country tunes, Louvin Brothers, Bill Monroe, that kind of stuff. We had been singing together for about a year before that.

His brother Steve Gore played in a bluegrass group called the Weedpatch Boys with Marvin Hedrick, Charlie Percifield and Jim Bessire (Jack's half-brother).

Steve played guitar in that band and he had all these lyric sheets and recordings of people like the Louvin Brothers, Bill Monroe, that kind of stuff.

So Dave and I started singing those things; he took the tenor and I took the lead and we've been the Everly Brothers of Brown County ever since.

Dave got a guitar in the fall of 1963. He bought himself a Gibson 12-string when he was a junior in high school. I thought, "Well, hell, if he can do it, I can do it."

So, about February of '64, I went down to Tom Pickett's music store in Bloomington and bought a Harmony Classical nylon string guitar with case and instruction booklet, and I took it from there.

The folk music revival was in full swing; Joan Baez, Peter, Paul and Mary, The Kingston Trio, The Chad Mitchell trio. Roger McGuinn, who founded the Byrds was a banjo player for the Chad Mitchell Trio. They were on the "Hootenanny" TV show.

Circa 1964-65

The year after I got out of school, I had got to be friends with Jeff Bainter, he had been on the track team with me. He turned me on to Bob Dylan. He got us tickets to see the Kingston Trio at the IU auditorium. They put on a really good show.

I also saw Peter, Paul and Mary up at Clowes Hall.

I saw The Association open for the Lovin' Spoonful. "Along Comes Mary" was climbing up the charts (1966). I was blown away by the Association, they were flashy. The Lovin' Spoonful put on a good show too.

While we were still in school, Leon Pittman and I had this kind of quasi-Dixieland band called, of all things, "The Teen Beats". We had been in the high school band together; I played clarinet and Leon was a trumpet player. We had Don Davis, who was a trombone player, Mike Robertson and Bobby Eads played saxophones and Grover Moore played a Sousaphone.

27

We did a few things in the school arena.

After graduation, I was working in Muncie. My uncle, my dad's brother Ralph, got me a job on a road location survey team. I was hired on in the fall of 1963 as a "rod man," an engineer's assistant.

We surveyed for the I-69 bypass around Muncie. Twelve miles. I walked every inch of it. Standing out in ten-degree weather holding a transit rod, just waiting to see that orange flag off in the distance waving at me. Then I'd hold the thing up so they could take a measurement.

Of course, I also cut brush.

One time we had to go right through this hog lot on this farm, and there was this pool there with pigshit in it. And I had to lean out over the edge of that pool to hold a level rod, nothing holding me up but that rod, so they could get a reading. I'll never forget that.

I was making good money for 1963 - 225 dollars every two weeks, plus mileage. I was living with my folks on weekends.

I'd drive up early Monday morning, four or five o'clock. We stayed in this motel, got a group rate. Then drive back to Nashville on Friday evening, go to a ball game or whatever.

Not so bad for an 18 year old. I was driving a 1963 Corvair with a car payment of 81 dollars a month. I got 98,000 miles out of it before it finally died. The girls loved that car.

I was home one weekend and Leon came up to me and said,

"I heard you picked up guitar."

Part Two –

Join together with the band

Early Bands

"You guys are good,
but do you have to play so loud?"

I hooked up with Leon and Jerry Pittman in 1964, we were called The Mystics. That was the first rock band in Brown County that I knew of.

Jerry was the drummer and Leon, who played trumpet in the high school band, had taken up the bass guitar. Don Davis, who had also been in the high school band, played guitar and I played guitar and sang.

They wanted to call it "The Fabulons". I didn't like that, I thought it was hokey. So Leon named us The Mystics. I found out later there was a band out of Louisville, a show band that played college gigs, also called The Mystics.

I thought at first we were just going to be an instrumental group, and I was going to be the rhythm guitarist. But then Leon said, "Do you sing any songs?"

I think he knew that the girls and Dave and I had been singing. "Johnnie B Goode" had been covered by Dion, and I had heard it on the radio a couple of times and somehow I had managed to learn the lyrics, so I said, "I can sing Johnny B Goode".

We were off and running. I started learning songs, this would've been the Spring or late winter of 1964.

We played at DeMolay dances, at the Masonic Lodge, we played at high school dances after ball games, homecoming, stuff like that.

We did the songs of the day and recent past like "Little Latin Loopdeeloo" by the Righteous Brothers, before their really big hit, which was "Unchained Melody". Lots of Doo-wap, R&B and Soul kind of stuff. We did "Walkin' the Dog" by Rufus Thomas "Twist and Shout", and "Tossin and Turnin'" by Bobby Lewis out of Indianapolis.

I think we did a couple of rockabilly songs. We did five or six songs, at the most.

Then the Beatles hit and I just fell in love with the Beatles. I was enthralled with the Beatles, I just loved those guys. To this day, I still do.

So we started doing some Beatles songs like "I Should Have Known Better".

Don Davis didn't last too long, two or three months. I think it might have been too rock'n'roll for him. He was more country. He ended up being primarily a steel guitar player.

We started doing fraternity dances down at IU.

Leon and Jerry and I, The Mystics, played at a Democratic Party rally out at somebody's farm for 25 dollars. I think Lee Waltman lined it up for us. That would've been 1964.

We ran our only microphone through Leon's Silvertone bass amp. It sounded terrible. But, you know, for these local characters, they appreciated it. For 25 bucks, what are you gonna ask?

We did that for a while. Dr. Schneider's son, Rick, who was like, 16, played keyboards for us for a while after Don Davis left.

Bands were wearing matching outfits in those days. I remember Bill Haley and the Comets, those guys were wearing suits, back in the '50's. Louie Jordan and Big Joe Turner - they all dressed alike.

At one point we had these black turtlenecks and red cardigan sweaters, black pants and black shoes. And then we got a little more casual and we got these blue chambray work shirts with a pair of jeans and some kind of nice-looking shoes.

I've got pictures somewhere.

And then the Beatles came along with these high-heeled boots and the collarless jackets – wow! Then the Nehru thing. I had a Nehru jacket that was multi-colored, it was very pretty.

Steve Duckett was the last addition to The Mystics, at the very tail end of that he did a few shows with us playing rhythm guitar.

We were booked for a high school dance and I had strep throat and I couldn't sing, and Dave stepped in because he'd been in a band in Terre Haute called Madras. They were pretty good. A really good cover band, and Dave was the out-front singer.

I played lead guitar and was not very good, Rick Snyder was on the electronic organ, which is an important part on songs like "96 Tears" and "Hanky Panky" by Tommy James.

We finally split up around 67 or 68, I think.

"Sons of Manitou" alumnus Tom McManus and I reconnected in 1966, he was a second lieutenant in the army getting ready to go to Vietnam, I was getting ready to go to boot camp in the Naval Reserve.

He was coming in from Fort Sill, Oklahoma and he had a Datsun 2000 sports car, what became Nissan later on. Nobody around here had ever heard of those things.

I had about three weeks before I had to report to the Great Lakes Naval Training center. Tom had just finished artillery school and was getting ready to go to Georgia and then Vietnam.

He said, "Listen, I'm going to see my mother and my brother before I ship out, why don't you come with me to New York for a couple of days?" So, we did.

We took the scenic route, we followed the Ohio River through southern Ohio, West Virginia, we got on the Pennsylvania Turnpike, got into rush hour traffic in New York City at six in the morning.

And then we went out, and we boogied for three days. And then I flew back from Kennedy.

Later on, Tom showed up after he'd done his tour-and-a-half. He was a forward artillery spotter. And he did 18 months in country.

He came back through, his hair had grown, he'd become a musician. Eventually we lost track of each other

About 1966-67, I can't remember exactly, but I heard about these guys from Bloomington who were trying to form a band. I was hooking up with some Bloomington kids, I was sorta

34

kinda dating a gal over there, and I connected with some of these people.

A guy named Charles Whaley, a drummer, was really hot to get this band together and these guys had heard about me, I think through the fraternity house circuit that we played a lot with the Mystics.

I hooked up with them and we did the same circuits as "East-West Wire Service". Bill Barnes was on keyboards, Glen Riggs was on bass, me on rhythm guitar and vocals.

We went through several different lead guitar players. John Patton was one of them. He was later on with a group called "The Misery Brothers" out of Needmore and Unionville. They were fun. They had a rhythm guitar player and singer named Omar Hudow, he was a character, a really neat guy.

We (East-West Wire Service) went to the Battle of the Bands at the Indiana State Fair, but we didn't win. If I recall correctly, the winner was a band called Sounds Unlimited which later became Mason Profit. And their drummer, Art Nash, eventually became part of String Bean String Band.

Then, we kind of split up, the first version. I was living here in Brown County and just floating around and jamming a little bit. I didn't even have much of a repertoire at that point, I was just spaced out...

Charles Whaley and I got to be really good friends. I've lost contact with him, but I saw him maybe 15 years ago. Last I knew, he was living in Bowling Green, Kentucky.

In 1967 Danny Kummer had an apartment in Bloomington. I used to go over to there before and after gigs and get stoned. We got tickets to see Peter Paul and Mary at the IU auditorium.

When Gene McCarthy was running for President (1968) they had a big rally, a bunch of people on Dunn Meadow: Peter,

35

Paul and Mary, Phil Ochs, and Tom Lerher, an ex-Harvard math professor turned humorist.

My folks always encouraged my music. Sometimes they didn't especially like the kind of music I did, but about 1970 my dad came to hear this one band I was in with Dan Groves "Beggar's Opera", at a homecoming dance in the high school 'cafetorium'.

High school dance in the BCHS "cafetorium"

He said, "You guys are good, but do you have to play so loud?"

He didn't particularly care for my lifestyle, which at that time was smoking pot and taking psychedelics, and later I got heavy into alcohol.

Mom got to hear some of my early recording efforts, demos and so on.

I don't think Pop ever did. He died in 1972. On Laura's 21st birthday. She found him in the kitchen, he was getting ready to go to work. Massive heart attack. He was a big influence on my music. I miss him.

I wish he could have heard some of the String Bean stuff we did. Also the My Brown County Home thing. I think he

36

would have been impressed. He would've loved that. He loved Brown County, never wanted to live anyplace else.

He and I were up and down in our relationship. He was an alcoholic. But he died sober. His last four or five years, he was sober.

He was a true Brown County boy, what John Sisson calls "a hill ape". That's the folks I know, I run with, all us Brown County characters, we're hill apes. That's our tribe.

Cardboard Zombies

"And that is just a fraction of
all the bands I've ever been in..."

After East-West Wire Service had broken up and gone our separate ways, in the late fall/winter of 1967-68, I moved to Terre Haute.

Dave Gore and Steve Duckett had both gone there to study at Indiana State University, and I wanted to form a band with them.

I was living in this communal house, a big three story Victorian house, there must have been eight or ten of us living there. I was sleeping in the basement with a second cousin of mine, Gary Deaver.

I wanted to do a band, but I needed an income, so I applied for a job as a stock boy in some downtown department store. On Friday, I had gotten word to show up for a job the following Monday. So, on Saturday I thought I'd better come back to Brown County to see my friends and family, because I was going to be busy in Terre Haute and I might not see them for a while.

I went out to my brother's house, he was renting a little place with Lance McDonald out on old 46 that was owned by Von Williamson.

They were having a party, a bunch of guys sitting around smoking dope and drinking beer. There was an older guy named Dallas Stiles, he was always at the core of these pot parties. I walked in and everybody was stoned out of their mind, and so I got stoned myself.

Dallas said, "Are you looking for a gig?", and I said "Yeah, I am" and he said "There's this club up in Fountain Square (Indianapolis) called "Le Scene" where all the teenage hippy crowd hangs out."

It was owned and run by a guy who had been a dancer in New York.

Dallas said, "There's an audition tomorrow up there, this group has lost their singer and they need a lead singer."

The group was called "The Cardboard Bachs".

The leader of the band was a keyboard player named Rick Durett He loved Mozart, Handle, Haydn, that stuff. Early Classical and Baroque.

I went in and auditioned and I got the job, out of eight or ten people.

We rehearsed the next day for like 14 hours or something. And the *next* day, I was the out-front lead singer for The Cardboard Bachs in some club in Louisville.

I was 22 years old at the time. What a trip!

I sang 14 songs, and the keyboard player covered the three or four others that we did.

It was Winter of 1968, because I remember this Florida girl came back up to Indy with us and she had never seen snow before.

So, we went down to Nashville, Tennessee, actually, Franklin, which is a suburb. I stayed with Rick Durett, the keyboard player, who was basically the leader of the band. The other guys in the band were from Tennessee as well, except for the lead guitar player – he was an Indiana boy.

Then, we went down to Jacksonville, Florida. What had happened was, we had been farmed out by this Indianapolis booking agency to a group in Jacksonville, Florida.

And we hooked up with this guy, and he said, "You guys are going to be the new Zombies." They had split up, and he had booked us as the "re-formed Zombies". He was a real con man.

And we had to fake British accents. And we did it. I was "Robin Bee", that was my stage name. Sounded more British.

The bass player refused to go along with it, so if anybody asked, we'd say, "Oh, we had to pick up this American bass player."

And we did Zombie songs - "Tell Her No", "She's Not There". And some other things. This was before their comeback when they did "Time of the Season".

We toured all over the deep South, all around, for months. We played in Northern Florida, Tennessee, Georgia, South Carolina, all up and down the Gulf coast, Jackson, Mississippi, Thibodaux and New Orleans, Louisiana, East Texas. It was a trip.

Rick had a Dodge van and we hauled all the equipment in a U-Haul trailer in the back. The van was painted psychedelic and we were crammed into this thing, the four of us and a roadie.

We did some shit. We had rednecks in north Florida throw beer bottles at us. And I ended up, Robin Bee from the new Zombies, signing autographs! Shirt cuffs!

One time we played three gigs in one day; we went from Sarasota to Pensacola to one other little town on the Gulf coast of Florida. We were so stoned at that point from driving, the drummer put the wrong beat on this one song by the Zombies. It was a train wreck, but we got through it.

The show must go on.

We had a road manager named Leaf, she and I really hit it off. I was the only one she would sleep with on the road, because she knew she could trust me, I wouldn't try anything sexual with her. The other guys...? She was really a beautiful lady.

Rick had an *actual* carboard box full of his classical records and a small record player. We would check into a motel and he would listen to that classical music. It was a trip.

In 1968, we played with Vanilla Fudge at the Lousiana State University Auditorium. They had kind of a psychedelic soul sound. They put on a great show. There were four of them, mostly guitar, organ, bass and drums. The drummer and bass player went on to hook up with Jeff Beck and became Beck, Bogart and Appasee. They put a couple of albums out.

We did that tour, drove back to Indianapolis from Beaumont, Texas, and that's the last gig we did on that tour.

A couple of days later, we were back at our home base, Le Scene, warming up for the Yardbirds with Jimmy Page.

I remember giving Keith Relf, the lead singer, two cigarettes, because he was out. They didn't carry any money with them, they had handlers.

He had an abscessed tooth, and I had these muscle relaxers for these spasms in my back. So Shawn Jones, our lead guitar player, approached me and said, do you think you could give Keith a couple of those muscle relaxers, because he's in pain, so I did.

And Shawn sat back in the dressing room and traded licks with Jimmy Page.

Relf was just this little guy, about 5'5", but he had this great big voice. They were really nice guys. The bass player was really nice. The drummer was an asshole. Just a jerk. But Jimmy Page was really nice. And of course, within the next year, Led Zeplin was formed.

They put on a great show. They used some of our amplifiers.

We also warmed up for The Electric Prunes who had that song, "I Had Too Much to Dream". They were nice guys from California.

So, we were stuck in Indianapolis playing these really crappy gigs. The booking agency that we had, the one that had farmed us out to the guy in Jacksonville, wanted Rick, our keyboard player, to play with the Olivers, a group out of Fort Wayne that was really hot in those days.

So, that was the end of the Carboard Bachs. The Tennessee boys went back to Tennessee, and I went back to Brown County.

Shortly thereafter, we reformed the East-West Wire Service with a couple of new guys and we got some good gigs and played around quite a bit.

The original line up was Bill Barnes on keyboard, Charles Whaley on drums, me on guitar and Glen Riggs on bass.

The second version was John Patton on lead guitar, me on second guitar, Charles on drums. We had a bass player for a while that didn't work out, so we went to a three piece and I went to bass. Then we picked up a guy from South Bend who had transferred to IU, Drew Milligan, and he took over bass and I went back to guitar. Later on, George Fryback played drums.

That lasted for a year or two and then I quit.

That's kind of the progression of that particular musical epoch...

And that is just a fraction of all the bands I've ever been in...

In the late 60's, I started writing some songs, some little nonsense things.

I had one little song, it was kind of self-serving, called "I Haven't Quite Figured It Out". It was a decent song and in the early String Bean days, we did that song.

In 1970, prior to String Bean, I was hanging out at Clifford Brown's house out on Lower Owl Creek with Jim Tracy and some other hippy-type folks from Needmore, and I wrote this song called "Smiles".

I was enamored with a lady named Barbara Campaign, whose father was one of the developers of Crest toothpaste. A chemist from IU.

I fell for Barbara, whose nickname was "Boo", and so I became "Bo" I wrote this song in unrequited love for Barbara Campaign. It's called "Smiles", it's on my album. And people to this day still ask for that song, I've had other musicians say, please give me a chart for that song"

It's my theme song, I guess, along with "Alive and Pickin'" by Tom McCormick from Arizona.

Part Three:

String Bean String Band

String Bean String Band

"Hey, remember me?"

About 1970-71, I was involved with a group out of Bloomington called "Cottonmouth" with a drummer and a lyricist I had jammed with named Kevin Tier. He called me one day and told me Bob Stoner was leaving the band and they needed a rhythm guitarist and singer.

John Ory Stith was the bass player. He's a legendary Bloomington bass player who has played with everybody around here. Patrick Calahan played lead guitar. I played rhythm guitar and sang along with Nick and Vicky Zellinger. We had really good three-part harmonies. Nick played rhythm guitar and keyboards and Vicky just sang.

Later Vicki sang a song Kenny and I wrote, "Sail On" for the Bloomington Sampler, a record showcasing local singers.

49

She had heard it live at one of our shows. She sang lead with String Bean backing. I think it's one of the best recordings we ever did. Art did a wonderful job on drums.

Cottonmouth played almost exclusively original material, so we didn't get that many gigs. But we practiced almost every week and drank a lot of beer and shared our songs that we had written.

I think I left Cottonmouth because I was really getting into the country aspect of music.

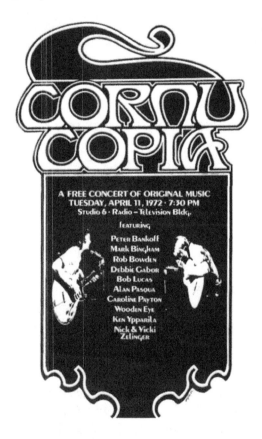

WTIU out of Bloomington did a singer/songwriter show and Nick and Vicky asked me to join them for that and we did my song "Smiles" and a couple of other tunes.

And they invited this friend of theirs from Ball State named Kenny Ypparila, a kid maybe 17 or 18 years old, to come down and play fiddle and mandolin with us on this TV show.

Nick and Vicky and Kenny and I did that TV show in April 1972, then in July or August, we had this Sunday jam going out behind what was then Grasshopper Flats, the pagoda building. It was just a gravel lot with a couple of benches there, and a bunch of local folks would show up.

During that summer, John Sisson had introduced Dave and I to Paul Pell, a banjo player, and Paul and Dave and I, and occasionally someone else sitting in, would jam and all kinds of people would show up.

The Grasshopper Flats jams - Summer 1972

People would sing along and play shakers – baby food jars full of popcorn, or play spoons or whatever.

And we were playing one Sunday and Kenny Ypparila came walking down the street, on the east side of Van Buren street, with a fiddle case in his hand and a girl named Jill, a folk singer and guitarist, holding her guitar case.

They had been up to the Old Hickory (now "Out of the Ordinary") to audition and got turned down because they were too Folkie. The Old Hic wanted Country.

I saw Kenny and I said, "Hey, remember me?" and he said, "Yeah!"

I said, "Come join us!"

And they came and joined us. And after a couple of weeks of that, we got to talking; there was Paul, there was Dave, there was me, there was Kenny – we said, "Let's make a band!"

And so we did.

Somewhere after a couple of rehearsals Kenny said, "We need a bass", so I said, "I'll try it."

I had dabbled in bass. I had messed around with it, but I didn't know much about it.

So Kenny and I went out and bought a used Kay electric bass guitar for 25 bucks, and split the cost. The pick-up wasn't even picking up the G string. So I had an E and an A and a D.

So I learned to play bass on three strings. Until we finally got enough money together that I eventually got a Gibson EB3, a solid body bass. I used that for a couple of years until I got a 1966 Fender Precision, which is THE bass, as far as I'm concerned.

So we went up to the Old Hickory, where Kenny was turned down a few weeks before, and we got the job.

We were running a PA with two microphones through a Fender Bandmaster guitar amplifier, and the amp broke down, so we just did it acoustically. Unplugged.

We got the gig. Every Friday night, fifteen bucks apiece and all the beer we could drink.

It was September of 1972. We started out on Friday nights and after a few weeks they gave us Wednesday as well, so we did two nights a week. It was Dave, Kenny and me on vocals, so we had nice three-part harmonies and we all sang lead as well.

It was Paul Pell on banjo, Dave Gore on guitar and vocals, me on bass and vocals, Kenny Ypparila on fiddle and mandolin and later steel guitar.

String Bean at the Old Hickory 1972

Kenny taught himself to play steel while we were playing the Old Hickory. He bought himself a Harlin Brothers six-string multi-chord, which was probably the easiest to learn on. Then he moved on to a ten-string Fender, which he played for years.

The Old Hickory shows turned into a wild weekend scene, with people lined up down the block every Friday night.

I tell you, we packed the place. Everybody in Brown County was there. The place was full of red necks from Columbus and hippies from Bloomington.

53

Here were the two main subcultures of our society, the red necks and the hippies and there wasn't a harsh word ever that I could remember, nothing approaching a fight, which in some redneck bars at that time probably would have happened.

No fights, no bad vibes at all between the hippies and the rednecks. The music brought all these people together.

I think we kind of took them by surprise. They were probably expecting George Jones and Merle Haggard and we gave them pretty stuff, old time mountain music, and stuff from some of the hippie rock bands who had gone back to old time country music.

String Bean String Band

"Will the Circle Be Unbroken" was the core of the music movement of that time, and we did a lot of stuff from that album, which had been organized by the Nitty Gritty Dirt Band. That kind of music was really coming on in the pop sphere.

We did several instrumentals like "Soldier's Joy", songs by Bill Monroe and Doc Watson. Old fiddle tunes. Stuff from "Sweetheart of the Rodeo" by the Byrds. Flying Burrito Brothers. "Up on Cripple Creek". Stuff like that. A couple of Porter Waggoner songs; we kicked off the show with "Howdy, Neighbor, Howdy".

Eventually we did an atomic version of "Orange Blossom Special" which went on for six, eight, ten minutes. We jammed out. We were all stoned in those days. The crowd was whooping and hollering, snake dancing around the place. It was a trip.

People would come over from the Playhouse after the show to get a drink, tourists from out of town. "What is going on here?"

It was a happening, it really was.

One night as we were going on break, this middle-aged tourist couple asked us, "Who are you guys? Where did you come from?"

Here were these guys with hair down to their shoulders wearing cowboy shirts and blue jeans, and cowboy boots, singing old-time country songs and mountain music.

"Oh, we're from around here and Bloomington."

"Are you professors of folk music?"

"No, Dave's a carpenter and I'm a housepainter. Kenny's a student."

55

They just thought we were really something.

It was a special time. People were getting along better.

I remember when pot-smoking locals were working for and with beer-drinking good old boys on construction sites and God knows what all and nobody gave a damn about appearances. We were all Brown Countians. We were a cosmopolitan little cell in what is, aside from Bloomington, the middle of Good Ol' Boy land.

This place is just special.

Ernie Pyle compared it to Martha's Vineyard and other places that have a special vibe that attracts special people. Even back when Hohenberger called the locals "rustics", the rustics and the artists got along fine.

In the very beginning there was a dentist here in town named Stu Flights, originally from Carmel, and he really liked the band and he even bought us a small PA.

That's how we got into that circuit up in Indianapolis. Stu Flights said, "I've got this booking agent friend up in Indianapolis, and I'm going to try to get him down here."

And it took him about a month. Then Alan Deck comes down and hears us, and he says, "I can book you guys."

Alan Deck was a media guy, he had a degree in radio and TV broadcasting, he had a radio program, he taught audio-visual courses at Butler University, which was his alma mater.

With Paul Pell, String Bean String Band 1973

He put us on that circuit of supper clubs and steak houses, Stable Innfluence, Flaming Hearth Restaurant, Cattleman's. That's the circuit we were on in the early 70's. A college gig now and then, Butler (University), wherever.

During that supper club circuit time, we all had girlfriends. And they would play spoons and we called them "The Spoonettes". While we were up on stage playing they'd be out there dancing and playing spoons. All beautiful girls. Just knockouts.

We did our first concert as String Bean at the gymn at Franklin College, opening for David Bromberg, a folk/bluesy guy who was a pretty big name back in those days. He seemed like a nice enough guy.

57

Backstage at David Bromberg show

We did our first four-song demo with Rich Fish on a Teac four track recorder in his living room. I think he was a grad student at IU at the time. Then, shortly after that, he came to the Old Hickory and recorded one of the performances we did there.

THE STRINGBEAN STRING BAND

I did a demo for a commercial out of TRC, Talun Recording Company, with Gary Shatzlein up in Indianapolis, but they didn't use my vocal. He did the second demo we did. The first studio demo we did at TRC with Gary, we did a song I wrote in 1970 called "Smiles".

In September of 1973 we did a job at the old Bush Stadium baseball park, the "Indy-an Summer Concert" with the Nitty Gritty Dirt Band, John Hartford, John Stewart, the Dillards, The Wright Brothers Overland Stage.

It was billed as "Sophisticated Bluegrass" Somewhere along there we started using the slogan, "Progressive Country In Overdrive".

After about a year and a half, we had a regular booking in Louisville and Dave just didn't want to travel. So he gave his notice.

We did a week at the Regulator, now Kilroy's Sports bar, this would be 1973, I guess. We rented tuxedos for the Saturday night, Dave's last night, and they were each a different color. Colored tuxedos were in in those days.

59

In Tuxedos at The Old Regulator

In February of 1974, we were booked for two shows at the Rivoli Theater on East Tenth Street in Indianapolis, opening for Roger McGuinn.

In between the first and second show, Scot, our banjo player asked McGuinn if he would come up and do a song with us. And they came up with "You Ain't Going Nowhere", a Bob Dylan song which the Byrds did on "Sweetheart of the Rodeo".

I think he was a little hesitant, but he agreed to do it, but he didn't know what to expect. I don't know how much of us he had heard prior to his show.

He came out and Kenny had the steel guitar licks for the intro down, and then we jumped into the song, and Kenny and I had the harmonies.

He looked over at me like, "You guys really know what you're doing," and he just grinned. His expression looked like, "This is going to be fun."

When the song was over he kind of gently slapped me on the shoulder as if to say, "good job" and walked offstage.

A very nice man, very nice. He was just a great down-home guy. I've always admired his music, and he was just the nicest fellow. Not spoiled by fame.

I've always loved the Byrds.

At Nashville's Village Green gazebo

Crowd at Village Green gazebo

Dave Gore's parents (top) and Robbie's mom (center) were in the crowd at the Village Green performance.
(Brown County Democrat photos)

On the Road

I wish I could remember all the stories…

Dave and I were drawn to Bob Cheevers through Nancy Stouffer, who was Nancy Cheevers at the time. Bob came back here with her and started booking gigs.

We started playing together, trading songs and what not. Bob would get a pizza joint gig or a coffee house gig or something and Dave and I would join him for part of his show. That was the summer of 1972.

He eventually joined String Bean.

Paul Pell played the old fashioned frailing style claw hammer banjo but we were starting to drift more for a pop/country, country rock kind of sound. The Nitty Gritty Dirt Band were electrified and they could play bluegrass or they could play folk rock, country rock kind of stuff. Paul left the band because his playing was somewhat limited and we were expanding our horizons.

We auditioned three or four people to take Paul's place and we finally settled on Scot Merry, who could also play bass. That opened me up to play harmonica and rhythm guitar on some things where the banjo wasn't necessary.

Bob could play some rudimentary drums, and he started to play a little bit of drums on the more rock-oriented stuff. But he also played rhythm guitar on some original songs.

About 1973, we were playing at a place called the Stable Influence up on 86th and Ditch in Indy.

A guy named Tom Norman approached us and said he was with the drummer from Mason Profit, did we think we could get him up to play some? We said, "Sure". I think he had dragged Art there because he wanted him to hear us.

I had seen Art in his first band, Sounds Unlimited, which became Mason Profit, back when they were all just teenagers, a bunch of high school kids, and I was impressed with Art's drumming even then.

Art Nash in Mason Proffit

So he came up. He was drinking G&T's, and I think he had a pretty good buzz. And he played at concert volume, too loud for this little bar and club, because he was used to playing

64

big halls and everybody being electrified. He was playing like everything was electrified. We were still playing with these small pick-ups, these little Barcus Berry pickups not even as big as a domino, and running through a small PA.

But we asked him if he would consider joining the band. Mason Profit had broken up by then (1973). He said, "I've got to go back to LA and tie up some loose ends and I'll be back and I'll do a week with you" – I guess it was at the Regulator. He did the week and then he decided he'd stay with us for a while, and of course, he stayed with us 'til the end.

Bruce McConnell was getting involved with us pretty good by then. He went out and got these big pieces of plexiglass and put them around Art's drumset because he was too loud for us. Art wasn't very happy about it. Finally, we got over that because we didn't want to lug that thing around on the road. We updated our electronics and our sound equipment instead.

We'd still do these old traditional instrumental things with an electric bass and drums. Like "Orange Blossom Special" – we really jammed out on that one. Also things like Salt Creek,

65

Scotland and some bluegrass tunes, but with drums. We'd rock out on these old country instrumentals and people liked it.

Alan Deck, our manager at the time, had put together this real neat promo package. He's got a flair for that kind of stuff. He had a column in this entertainment publication out of Indianapolis and he had a radio show called "In the Dread of Night" where he played Reggae stuff.

He started researching where we might play; bluegrass magazines, music publications, booking agents, all kinds of different avenues. He sent this package off to every source of bluegrass and old time country music he could find.

An outfit called Ryle and Strauss out of Chicago picked us up and also Star Productions out of Minneapolis picked us up and they put us on the road.

Bob and Nancy split up and Bob left and went back to California.

We had replaced Dave with a guy named John Rau, who had been with a group called Lantern out of Bloomington, and they'd broken up. He didn't sing like Dave did, but he was a good lead player. He was with us for about a year, year and a half. He travelled with us all over the place.

Then John left the band and we went to a four-piece.

We went out on the road and we played all over the place.

We'd be out for three or four weeks at a time, maybe even six weeks sometimes. From Chicago, to Grand Forks, North Dakota, to Minneapolis to someplace in Iowa, someplace in Wisconsin, someplace in Michigan. We just bounced all around. We played the Chicago area quite a bit.

We played at junior colleges, bars, nightclubs, and a few concerts.

There was a Wisconsin group called Hartsfield that had some regional hits and we did a concert with them. We did a concert with a group called Zazu in Chicago. And we did some small college things just by ourselves.

We also did these showcase concerts. One was in Kearney, Nebraska and another was in Des Moines. These shows would have as many as ten or 12 acts and smaller colleges would come to these showcases to book entertainment for the next school year. We played at the National Entertainment Conference.

The van was this big box on the back of a double-tired rear end with all the equipment. Scott Merry had this hammock which he strung across and above the PA stuff in the back of the van and he would hang out there in the hammock. When it was daylight, he read.

We had this old couch that we'd put behind the two seats up in the cab of the van. There'd be somebody driving, somebody in the passenger seat, and the rest of us, except for Scott back in the hammock, would be on the couch.

It was an adventure. I was the oldest guy in the band once we had settled into the five of us travelling all over the place. I was 30, 31 32.

We played northern Minnesota and northern North Dakota in the dead of winter, travelling in that big box van, We'd just bundle up and head on down the road.

I wish I could remember all the stories...

We would check into a motel and say there were two of us. And then we'd all share one room. Some of us would have to sleep on the floor, but we had sleeping bags and things. We saved money that way.

Also, we would disconnect the odometer on the rental van. We'd drive from here to Grand Forks, North Dakota with the odometer disconnected.

67

We drove through blizzards that people died in. We drove through these snow banks in Minnesota and North Dakota, when it would just be blind whiteness for a second or two.

I remember one time we hit this snow bank and there was just a flash of white where you couldn't see the road or anything and Art Nash – he's kind of high strung anyway – he jumps up off the couch and said, "This is it!"

And after that, we would say that often, just to poke fun at him; "This is it!"

This neat old hotel is where we stayed in Grand Forks

We played this roadhouse outside of Breckenridge, Minnesota, which wasn't that much of a town. They had to move the pool table out of the corner so we could set up.

But in that same month, we might do a concert with some famous regional band, open up for them.

We'd go from moving-the-pool-table-out-of-the-corner-of-a-bar to a concert hall, a small auditorium somewhere with some group that was famous in the Chicago area or Minneapolis or whatever.

We played this place in Richmond, Kentucky that was called No Dogs Allowed. It had been a fancy nightclub upstairs,

68

and that was where we stored our cases and stuff, and we'd go up there to smoke joints and so forth. There were all these tables and chairs that had been sitting there gathering dust for years.

The bar was down in the basement, which was what was left of the establishment. Half the tile was off the floor and the back wall of the stage had all these water pipes and electrical wires running up and down. The lighting was one bare light bulb above the stage.

It was full of redneck hippies. Bib overalls, long hair and beards, that kind of thing.

And for four years we went all over the place; upstate New York, the Great Lakes States, the Great Plains States, the whole Midwest, part of the South. We played in Toronto, Canada.

In 1973 we did three bluegrass festivals in the East. We did one in a little town called Hallam, Pennsylvania, outside York, not too far from Washington, DC, so a lot of people and a couple of bands from DC showed up.

We shared the bill with Roland White, who was playing with The Country Gazette. He had taken up the guitar in honor of his brother, Clarence White, who had been in the Kentucky Colonels with Billy Ray Latham.

Also on the bill was the Country Gentlemen out of DC, with Charlie Waller. Their mandolin player was a young guy named Ricky Skaggs.

We got to be friends with the Buffalo Gals, an all-girl bluegrass band from Syracuse, New York. They were really good. Later, when I was living in Ohio, I came across this coffee table book, "The Women of Country" and there was a section in there on the Buffalo Gals.

Kenny and Nancy Josephson, their bass player had a little thing going. She ended up marrying David Bromberg.

Later that summer we went to Virginia. The Shenandoah River ran right to the edge of this campground, a festival grounds. Kenny and Nancy and I went skinny dipping in the Shenandoah. We swam across it and back.

In Virginia, we played on the same bill as Jimmy Martin, one of my favorite bluegrass singers of all time. I think he was great. The Osborne Brothers and Bluegrass Alliance were also at that show.

Our manager, Alan Deck, and I were sitting in a restaurant in Calloway, Maryland where we were going to do a festival, and Keith Case, a booking agent, walked in with Vassar Clements.

Allan said, "Do you have a band?", and Vassar said "No". Alan said, "Would you like to play with us?"

"Sure!"

It was Labor Day weekend and school had started, so the turnout wasn't that good and it was raining really hard, so instead of being in the open air, we went into this concrete block building and we did a set with Vasser. The next day we played outdoors.

Goosecreek Symphony was playing there too, with Bob Henke as one of their two lead guitar players. And when I met him in Phoenix later, I told him about that night and he thought that was pretty cool.

We were staying in the same motel as Vassar and a guy named Frank Wakefield, he was a mandolin player. And they came into our motel room and sat there and Vassar Clements, the fiddle player, played a guitar and Frank picked up Kenny's mandolin and they sat on the edge of the bed and we watched them play.

As far as I can tell, Vassar started out as a guitar player and then became a fiddle player for Bill Monroe. Frank Wakefield had played with Joan Baez in the early days with a group called the Greenbriar Boys.

It was incredible. The memory of sitting there and talking to Vassar Clements and watching him play guitar in some motel room. He was really good.

A really nice guy.

In the Summer of 1974 we played the Louisiana State Fair in Baton Rouge, opening for Dave Loggins ("Please Come to Boston") on Friday night and J.J. Cale on Saturday night. On Sunday night, we headlined.

We played on the same bill with Harry Chapin ("Cat's in the Cradle"), in Frankfort, Kentucky. I got to talk to him a little bit. He was a nice guy, but cocky, a New Yorker. But nice.

Peter Yarrow did not show – it was just Harry and us.

It was a trip. And that's how we lived for four years.

In between road trips with String Bean, we got together a band from Cottonmouth with Patrick and Vicki, Art on drums, Scott on bass and me on rhythm guitar, vocals and harmonica. There was also a little gal with a great big voice named Candy Pinkston.

Vicky and Candy and I had this great harmony on things like "Chain of Fools".

Patrick came up with that name, which is probably my favorite band name of all time, "The Half Astral Band".

It was a good band. We played the Bluebird and the Red Dog saloon; all the colored animal bars. Occasionally a fraternity dance or whatever.

Bob Lucas had been in a band called Goldrush, and about 1975-76, he approached us about joining, and we said, "OK!"

Kenny was playing lead at the time, we were down to four guys. Sometimes we'd play without a guitarist at all, just me on bass and harmonica, sometimes I would move over to rhythm guitar and Scott would take the bass and Kenny on fiddle, mandolin and steel, and some lead himself.

Bob added a whole bunch of stuff, all of his tunes and that voice. At that time, before he joined us, Kenny and I were the only two vocalists. We had a good sound, the two of us, but Bob added this high, wailing sound.

Right at the beginning of 1977 we got the call from Bruce McConnell, who had helped us out before.

Malibu and Thousand Oaks

"Let's not just do a demo, let's do an album…"

String Bean String Band ended up in California with the help of Bruce McConnell, who was a rich guy who liked the band. He took us out there, paid for a place for us to live, took us into the studio.

That was January of 1977, and we stayed there until almost Christmas of that year.

We were at a rehearsal with Bob Lucas at John Sisson's house out by Lake Monroe when Jim and Bruce called us up, and Bruce says, "I want to take you guys out West, to try and get a record deal."

Then he put Jim Moore on, and he says, "I'd really like to join you guys, I've always liked your band." And everybody said "Sure!", and so we took Jim on as pedal steel and dobro player.

We knew Jim through Bill Wilson. When Bill was playing that same supper-club circuit that we were in Indy, Jim was his lead player and steel player. We would go to see them sometimes or they would come to our gigs.

The reason we went to California was to try to get the big record deal. But first, we went to Colorado Springs, to this little eight-track jingle studio.

Our first engineer and co-producer, I guess you'd call him, was Bob Margouleff, and after a couple of days he was really frustrated with the equipment. He wanted something major.

At Indigo Ranch. Bob Margouleff at far left.

Margouleff and this British guy had come up with some kind of synthesizer combinations that Stevie Wonder was involved with. I remember him talking about working with Stevie. There's a long interview with him in the PBS History of Rock'n'roll series.

So Bob said, "Let's just take the whole band out to California. I know this 24-track studio out by Malibu where we should be able to get some good tracks."

76

And we all went to California...

Margouleff said, "Let's not just do a demo, let's do an album and then try and sell it to some companies."

So we did. Of course, he made more money that way.

We went into the Indigo Ranch studio and recorded ten songs right off the bat, forty minutes or so worth of material.

Before it was a recording studio, the Ranch, which overlooked the Malibu coast, had belonged to the Barrymore family. John Barrymore would go out there to dry out before an acting job. And John Barrymore, Jr. was in the same kind of way – it was the family curse.

California version number one

They had two techs who lived in a bunkhouse, a little cottage behind the main building. There was an in-house engineer, Richard Kaplan and his girlfriend, Lori Los Angeles. I

77

don't know if that was her real name or not. She was an artist, she did logo work for us.

Indigo Ranch was started by Mike Pinder, the original keyboard player for Moody Blues, and a guy named Michael Hoffman, a music and movie producer. I guess the Moody's did some of the tracks for their "Octave" album at Indigo Ranch.

They had this great big box, it was a "sound enhancer", it increased sustain and things like that; it beefed up the sound. It was huge, probably three feet by three feet by three feet. Of course, everything's miniaturized now, electronic, but for that ten-song album that we did, we used an "Aphex Aural Exciter".

Bob Lucas was with the band at that point. We did some of my songs, we did some of Bob's, a couple of old time instrumentals with a rock beat.

Art Nash was our drummer. He's an incredible drummer, but moody as hell. He used to break all the rules. Being the primary bass player, it was up to me to keep him under control.

Scot Merry, the second banjo player, did a really fine job on bass as well.

I played rhythm guitar quite a bit, and harmonica a bit. Bob was on lead, Art on drums, Kenny on everything. And Jim Moore on pedal steel and dobro.

So one day we were working a day session at Indigo Ranch, and Bob Lucas' son Noah, he was about five or six I guess, he was sitting in the control room chair, kind of pretending he was an engineer.

This tall skinny guy walks in with a shorter, stockier guy. And the tall skinny guy says,

"It's about time we got a decent engineer in here."

It was Neil Young and his manager.

So the next time we were there, we said, "How did it go with Neil Young?" And they said, "Good", he stayed there most of the night, just him and an acoustic guitar, he demo'd a bunch of songs."

When we went out to our cars to go home, there was a '58 Cadillac, primer gray, top down. I just happened to look inside, I was curious to see what he might have in his car. There was a flannel shirt, some newspapers and a half a six pack of Budweiser tall boys.

Stringbean/Buckdancer Cali '77

So, we did that (ten-song) album and started sending it out.

We did an audition for Kip Cohen, who was one of the big dogs at A&M records. He liked our sound, but he didn't think that we were commercial. The big band that hit during that time was Dire Straits, on Warner Brothers/Reprise, I think it was.

The way I remember it, Bruce wanted one of the big five: Warner Brothers, RCA, Capitol, A&M, Columbia, somebody like that. I think some people at United Artists were interested in us, but he didn't want to deal with them because they were a less-major label.

They probably would have put us on one of their little subsidiaries anyway, but what the hell? I mean, we had all of this material. And a certain stage presence, a certain energy.

But, whatever. You know, it is what it is...

And it was what it was...

We kept recording. We went back into the studio and did some more of Bob's stuff, a song of mine. A song Kenny and I wrote on the road, "Gypsy".

"Travelling by night
"And all through the day
"A thousand miles
"Just to get out and play
"White lines and highway signs
"Another chance just to run away"

"Chicago then Denver,
"Places in between
"Bright lights and all nights
"Rambling country scenes

"Wayfaring gypsy travelling free
"How long will it last?
"How long will it be?

"Sleepy towns and barroom clowns
"And nothin' much to do
"Highway sounds spinning around
"I got them motel TV blues
"But there's sun up in the mountains
"And cities in the rain
"Sometimes it's never ending

80

"And then I'm heading home again

I like that song

And you can take a double meaning on those white lines. We were mostly smoking pot, but every once in a while somebody would get hold of some coke or speed or something, us crazy hippies.

Even after we went to California, we played out. We played a little concert at a bar close to campus at the University of California, Davis.

We played several places in San Francisco, and up in the wine country, Marin County, out in there.

We made one last demo.

We were staying at a place outside of Thousand Oaks, in Ventura County, Adolph's Hidden Valley Ranch. It was a seven-bedroom Spanish villa mansion that was owned by this company that rented it out to visiting rock and pop stars. Joe Cocker stayed there during recording sessions.

There was a horse ranch right next to us. There was this big gathering room set above the three car garage. There was a pool. We had it made, I tell you.

We turned the gathering room into a studio, put some baffles around the drums and so on, instrument mics and what not.

We rented an 8-track recording machine. After having done all those recordings on the 24-track at Indigo Ranch.

There was a vestibule, a foyer area which we turned into the control room, with the board and the recording machine and so on. We had a nice mixing board that was part of our PA. And we recorded.

We had Kinky and Creeper with us at the time, two guys from Minneapolis that had been side men with Mason Profit when Art was with them. Kinky is Bob Schnitzer; Creeper is Bruce Kurnow; a couple of nice boys.

We did seven or eight songs, some things that Kenny and I wrote, some things that Kinky and Creeper wrote, this one instrumental called "Six a.m."

Creeper, besides playing keyboards, was a hell of a harmonica player. He could play harmonica and keyboards at the same time. He also played the concert harp and we used that on a couple of songs, including a song that I wrote called, "Just Another Dream".

He had a full-sized concert harp that we used in recording, but he also had a three-quarter-size electric harp made by Barcus Berry, the pick-up people. He played that at our gigs.

We called it quits just before Christmas time in '77. We had recorded, I don't know, thirty songs, something like that.

We ended up using a lot of that for the String Bean String Band reunion album, which started out at the Old Hickory with us playing "Up on Cripple Creek" and then into the Talun

82

Recording Studio /Gary Shatzlein sessions up in Indy, and then stuff we did out in California.

When we arrived in LA, it was raining.

That would've been late January, it was raining. Then, it hardly rained through that spring and summer and then, the day Elvis died (August 16, 1977), it rained in LA, which it hardly had at all.

And then, we were finished up at that villa, out in Thousand Oaks. All the furniture and stuff String Bean had was gone and I was loading up a few little things in my car and I was going to take off, head back to Indiana. This was just four or five days before Christmas of 1977.

Bob Cheevers showed up, he'd been in LA doing some things, and everybody was gone but me, I was just getting ready to leave, and he said, "I've got this idea for a song."

So we just sat on the floor, he had his guitar, and I threw out a bunch of suggestions, threw lines out to him, and we came up with this song called "There's a Girl in Amarillo". It was a complete song.

Later on, maybe eight or ten years ago, Bob was still in Nashville and he had a studio there and Dave and I went down there, he wanted us to sing background vocals on his "Texas to Tennessee" album, and we did "There's a Girl in Amarillo".

Bob sang the lead, of course, and Dave and I sang backgrounds on several songs.

That song just came to me this morning, it just hit me:

"There's a girl in Amarillo
"Eyes as bright as diamonds
"She never smiled for no one
"She's pumpin' gas and selling beer
"She fills your tank and takes your money

83

"Her lips must taste like honey
"But she hasn't kissed in years
"She's the last stop on that highway
"From here to Tucomcary
"They say she once was married..."

So, after we had written this song, I packed up and Bob went back to his LA friends, and as I was driving out of LA, it rained.

So, it rained when I came in, it rained when I left and it rained on the day of Elvis' death.

Bruce McConnell, our benefactor, the guy that spent all that money on us, he was supposed to shop that demo. We were all gonna go our own way and if Bruce got a nibble and something was going to happen we would get back together.

Bob Vernon, he was our road manager and sound man, he ended up in Vancouver as a sound and light man. Bob moved back to LA and became an assistant director for movies, videos and commercials. He did that for years.

Kenny stayed in Thousand Oaks, California, where we last lived, and he is there to this day. His wife is (the former) Gail Scrougham, Pete Scrougham's daughter, an old time Brown County family.

Scott stayed in LA for a while and ended up in Wisconsin, where he had spent his young years. He married, teamed up with his brother-in-law, and they moved to Nashville (Tennessee) and started a recording studio back during the 1980's.

Art and I came back to Brown County.

Part Four:

Brown County Interlude

BRD

"An ongoing series of near-misses"

Art and I came back to Brown County and got together with a friend of ours who was kind of hanging out with us named Kenny Stowell. He was a Carmel boy who had been in the Indianapolis music scene.

He rented Marie Goth's house there on 135 North from Kathy Noise, who was Eli Lilly's granddaughter. In 1978, we turned that place into a studio.

Richard Fish, who did the very first demo we ever did at the Old Hickory, had a production company out of Smithville, Indiana, just South of Bloomington.

Fish is a legendary local music producer and engineer, one of the founding spirits of WFHB Community Radio. When the comedy group Firesign Theater reformed and re-launched their career, he was their distributor.

He had this step-van with an eight-track recording board in it and we would pull up in the driveway behind the house, run a snake into the house and turn the house into a studio. And we recorded a bunch of stuff.

It was Kenny Stowell, Art Nash and me, with guests; Dave came in and did a couple of songs with us and Jim Moore played some steel. He had been with us for that year in California.

Jim Moore and Dave Gore and Kenny and Art and I were the core of that thing and we called it "Bird", "BRD". And I came up with a logo for it that was all triangles, the B was two triangles, and the R was a triangle with a leg coming down, and the D was just a triangle.

We put together a demo called "BRD at the Aviary". That was Kenny's idea.

Kenney was the most inventive guitar player I've ever worked with or even ever heard. He could play stuff that you just wouldn't believe. As good as anybody I've ever heard.

We sent out a few demos, if I remember right. But, nothing happened.

Bob Cheevers had a connection with a company out of London at the time and he did get this one four or five song demo to them that we called "Homegrown".

It got to London, and the A&R man, as they used to call them, said he liked the music. But the guys who owned the record company were Arab oil people and they wanted hits, commercial records that would sell millions of copies.

Our stuff was just a little too esoteric. Art Nash's lyrics were kind of strange. Some of the stuff was mine, Kenny and I wrote a couple of songs together.

We got a demo to London, anyway, but, you know, "An ongoing series of near-misses".

It's been the story of my life. Forever.

There's a line in my song "Smiles",

"Wishful thinkers sometimes say,"
"Things will surely turn out someday,"
"It'll happen anyway,"
"What am I to say?"

So many of us have had these near misses.

Well, Kenny Stowell moved away. I think he went to Texas. Art and I kind of floated around.

While we were doing that BRD thing, we had a group, Midnight Flyer. I was playing bass and Art was playing drums. That lasted a few months and we did quite a few gigs, and then, I'm not exactly sure what happened, that kind of faded, some of those folks moved away.

So I called up Jim Moore, who lived in Indianapolis at the time and said, "Lets form a duo". He knew some places we might be able to gig.

He played lead guitar and steel guitar and Dobro.

He had this wicked electric Dobro with a cast aluminum body, made in the 1930's. The volume control, you twisted the knob and it raised the pick-up closer or farther away from the strings. It was made by the Dobro company. I think at that time, in the late 1970's, it was worth $1,500. You run that through a Fender twin reverb amplifier and it just screamed. It was razzed out, it sounded wonderful.

I've got some demos we did in Nashville in 1991.

Jim said, "Let's get a bass player", so he called Butch Vernon, who had just left a group called Dusty Days that played the same circuit as String Bean up in Indy in the early 70's.

Then Butch said, "Let's get a drummer". So we got Donnie Weddle, who had just left Chooch and the Enchanters.

We called ourselves the Survivors.

That would be 1978.

We played around Indianapolis and Bloomington. It was a really fun band. Butch and I did all the singing, Jim played lead and steel, and I played second guitar, some harmony licks.

We did some country classics, but we had a rock edge to us. We did some classic rock and blues. We did some great versions of classic 50s and 60's rock. Like, "Young Blood" by the Coasters.

"I saw her standing on the corner,
"Yellow ribbon in her hair..."

You know, it's a dirty old man song...

We did "You Can't Judge a Book by Looking at the Cover" by Moze Allison. We did a version of "If Six Were Nine" by Jimi Hendrix; we'd get into a country beat with that razzed-out feel of Jim's dobro. It was a fun band. We did a couple of Stones songs, stuff like that.

We played around for a year and a half and somewhere in the summer of '79, Butch said,

"Boys, I'm sick of these Indiana winters."

He had spent two years in Scottsdale Arizona, and he knew some people there he had played music with.

So we picked up the band, girlfriends, wives, whatever, and we headed out West.

Part Five:

Western Swing

The World's Greatest Cowboy Band

"Black patent leather boots with white comets and stars going up the leg, and rattlesnake skin on the toes..."

So the Survivors picked up and moved to Phoenix.

I had a girlfriend who had moved to San Diego a few months before we moved out West. We'd try to get together as often as we could. I'd drive over there, stay for a few days. She was in El Cahone, which is part of the San Diego complex.

Butch called up this bass player friend of his who he'd played music with in the past, she was getting married and moving out of her place. The landlord had half a duplex right next door, so Donny, the drummer, and Penny, his wife, were right next door to Butch and I. Jim Moore and his wife Ann found a place not too far away. They had a pool, so we'd go over there sometimes.

Lance Fuqua was a drummer, somehow we got to know him and he told us about some places to play and Butch knew a few places.

That's when the World's Greatest Cowboy Band happened.

We knew somebody who was connected to these guys that were trying to put a band together for a show. It was a bunch of original songs for a show called "The Which Way Did They Go Medicine Show Featuring the World's Greatest Cowboy Band".

And that sort of absorbed "Survivors".

We had the costumes and everything, like, cowboy outfits.

Tom McCormick, who went by the name Tom E. Tucker - his wife, Carolyn, kind of made my costume. It was a black shirt with white piping. She put a bunch of rhinestones on the chest part above the piping. And there was 18 inch white fringe all up and down both arms and across the back.

This boot maker guy, somehow he ended up at the studio where we recorded our demos, I'm not exactly sure why, and he saw my costume and he said, "I'm going to make you a pair of boots to go with that costume".

And he did. Black patent leather with white comets and stars going up the leg, and rattlesnake skin on the toes. It was a really neat costume.

I had this black cowboy hat with a silver band and silver edging around the brim.

Tucker was kind of the front man, he did most of the emceeing and so on. He was an interesting character. He wrote almost all of the songs. I still do some of those songs. And we had skits as well.

He started out as a drummer, picked up the guitar, started writing songs. Later on, after I had moved back here, he picked up mandolin and washtub bass. He sent me a tape of his group, "The McNasty Brothers".

He had been a clown, and he'd been in those gunfight shows in tourist places like Tombstone, Frontierland, Virginia City.

There was the short-lived United Football League, and Phoenix had a team, and Tucker got the job as their mascot, a Yosemite Sam type. He looked like Yosemite Sam, with a big beard.

The idea was, The World's Greatest Cowboy Band would be a TV show. It was geared for television. It was a cowboy "Sha-Na-Na", if you remember that show.

We had some guys that were backing us, but I think they were drug dealers and they never followed through.

Tucker had this lavender-colored Nudie suit which was too big for him and these Spanish riding boots, high top cowboy boots with silver tips on the toes and this ten gallon Stetson hat with a purple hatband and two silver colored bull horns coming out of the hatband.

His character's name was Bull Thompson, an over-the-hill country singer who was playing bowling alleys and things like that. His friend Johnnie Robinson played Bull Thompson's brother-in-law and road manager, kind of an Elmer Fudd type character, Sidney.

He and Bull would get into these goofy discussions. There was this one song he wrote for this Bull Thompson character called "It Ain't Easy Being a Fallen Star".

"You might think I look like somethin' special,
"Maybe it's these fancy clothes I wear,
"But a busted heart don't know nothin' 'bout no
rhinestones,
"Inside I'm filled with hurtin' and despair

Here's the chorus –

"I got a phone and nobody calls me,
"My Cadillac's out of gas,
"If I don't pay up my rent next week,
"I'll be outta here on my backside,
"It takes about a pint of gin a day,
"Just to keep away the crazies ,
"It ain't easy, Bein' a Fallen Star"

On this one song Lucky Junior, Johnny, came out on roller skates and did rope tricks on roller skates.

Also, Tucker had an old Mexican character with a donkey called Old Rio. We pre-recorded the dialogue and played it through the PA, he just pantomimed, went through the motions.

Old Rio lights up a joint, takes a big drink of water - we had some things that we could make sounds that were supposed to be a flying saucer - so, this flying saucer lands close to Old Rio after he's gotten stoned.

That's the kind of stuff we did. It was fun.

It was a clever thing, it really was. Really good musicians. Tom was funny, creative, a real Renaissance guy.

We did an outdoor gig at one of the hotels and we did a gig for this gay group that were trying to raise money for some charity.

We did a run at a place called Johnny Below Zero's in Apache Junction. It's the town that is closest to Superstition Mountain. You go east through Mesa, which is one of Phoenix's connected cities, and Apache Junction is east of Mesa.

Colorado

"...we lived in a high mountain valley..."

The cowboy band was going nowhere - Butch had already left and gone back home to Indiana. There was hardly any money involved with the cowboy band. Once in a while Don Buzard's ex-wife would give us 50 bucks apiece or something.

Finally, the cowboy band faltered. Jim Moore wanted to get out of Phoenix and go to Colorado because his wife had a house there.

So in 1981-82, I moved to Colorado with Jim and Ann and we got together with a guy, Mike Prouty, who lived in Colorado Springs. He had worked with Bill Wilson when Jim was Bill Wilson's lead and steel player.

We were trying to get this band together. A friend of Jim's was a booking agent out of the Denver area. He had been in a group called Pleasant Street, which did the same circuit String Bean did in Indy.

Scott O'Malley was working at Stone County Booking Agency out of Greely, Colorado, near Denver. He got hold of Jim and said Billy Ray Latham was looking for a band. Latham had been in a group with Clarence White, who was with the second edition of the Byrds.

Clarence White was just a fantastic guitar player. He and his brother Roland White had been in a band that was in the first season of the Andy Griffith Show. Not the Dillards, who played the Darling Family; that was later.

They were called The Country Boys, but they ended up being called The Kentucky Colonels, with Clarence and Roland White and Billy Ray was their banjo player. He had a line in the Andy Griffith episode. He was a character. Then he was with the Dillards.

We did a show with them in Bloomington.

Billy Ray claimed Clarence was in on inventing this device, it was a stringbender that you put on a Fender Telacaster that bends the B string. That's how Clarence White got such a great sound when he was with the Byrds. It bends that B string up a half tone.

But Clarence White, he was unloading some equipment out of a van in Nashville (Tennessee), I guess he was pretty close to the street, and somebody hit him and killed him. He was like 27 or something. And he was just a monster guitar player.

So many sad stories.

So Billy Ray drove down from Denver to Jim's house and he said, "Let's give it a try," and he joined the band and we picked up a saxophone player named Bill Abeta. I was the bass player and principal singer.

We were called Buckdancer. That's actually what we were called in California. Bob Margouleff, our producer and engineer, didn't like String Bean String Band, he said it was hokey. So somebody came up with the word buckdancer, which means a street dancer back in the 1800's, like a Bojangles.

So Jim and I just used that name when we went to Colorado. That was the "Buckdancer II" band.

We played a lot, a lot of clubs and a couple of ski resorts. We did some original stuff and we did some Dire Straits, stuff like that. Some classic country. We did a little recording.

One day we were playing up in a little town called Cascade Falls in a little restaurant and bar called the Country Turtle. Mike Prouty, Jim Moore, me, Bill Abeta on saxophone and Billy Ray.

Scott Merry from String Bean String Band showed up. He had a band with his brother-in-law and wife. They played the officers club at Petersen Army Air base outside Colorado Springs.

He brought his banjo and he and Billy Ray traded licks, and it was great, the crowd really liked it. After Buckdancer II broke up, Billy Ray went out to California and formed a band called "Banjovi".

I was there for about a year and a half. We lived in a high mountain valley. You go up US 24 from Colorado Springs about

25 miles, it's called Ute Pass. Up above the town of Woodland Park. I bet we were at least 8,000 feet up. You look due south and there's Pike's Peak looming above you.

I lived with Jim and Ann in a large log house. Jim and I re-drywalled a couple of rooms and I did most of the painting. Jim and Ann's daughter Hannah was born there while I was living with them. I've got a picture of her and I sitting on the couch when she was just a baby, and then one of her and I sitting on a couch when she was about 18. She is gorgeous.

Jim and Ann Moore were back here a week or two ago (2019) and Ann showed me a picture of Hannah now and she's almost 40. She's an athlete and she's drop-dead gorgeous. Five-ten and just a beautiful woman, a great gal.

I got asked to her wedding about 2011, 2012, but of course I couldn't go, I didn't have any money. Jim and Ann settled in Oregon years ago and I think the wedding was in Seattle.

We played a lot at this one restaurant and bar called Thunder and Buttons. And we did a thing in Denver, and we did a little recording and we played at some bars around.

We backed up this one girl singer, she wanted to do a demo. She wrote mostly kid songs and she used Buckdancer to back her up.

That lasted about a year and a half, 1981-82.

There was this gal, Jeanie, who was very interested in me, but, like a fool, I didn't go after her. I was still in connection with a lady named Marion who had lived with me during the String Bean days and went to California with me. We stayed in contact and she came to Colorado Springs a couple of times to stay with me.

I guess I just didn't want Marion to find out about Jeanie. Jeanie was hot. Marion was a brain, a real brain.

Ann had another house outside Colorado Springs and Jim wanted to get out of music for a while, he was tired of it, so in the Spring of 1982, I decided to go back to Phoenix.

The All Musician Orchestra

"Oh yeah, I played at the Little Nashville Opry."

The cowboy band had reformed, but with different people. I talked to Tom and he said, "Come join us, play guitar, harmonica, sing..." So I jumped in on rhythm guitar and we did a few gigs, made some demos.

Bob Henke had come to play lead guitar. He had been with Goosecreek Symphony, which was very successful, put out a few albums. After they broke up, Henke had joined Dr. Hook and the Medicine Show and co-produced some of their recordings.

Once again, the cowboy band didn't do so well. It couldn't support us. There were six or seven of us.

We got this girl singer, Carol Rae, from Iowa to sing with the cowboy band and she and I got to be pretty good friends.

One night we went to see John Hendricks of the '50's vocal trio Lambert, Hendricks, and Ross. I probably could have gotten lucky that night, with Carol, but, I don't know... She was young... I thought the working relationship would suffer.

105

I stayed in Phoenix for several more years.

After the cowboy band split up again, Bob Henke, the lead guitar player said, "You play bass, don't you? I'm going to put this trio together."

So Henke and I hooked up with a guy named Jim Moorehouse who had a recording studio in his garage at home. We demo'd a lot of stuff for a songwriter named Julie Speelman out of Phoenix.

I would drive over to her house and we would work on songs together and then we'd go into the studio. We recorded both stuff she wrote herself and songs co-written with me.

I also recorded a bunch of my stuff. I recorded this one song with Liza Martin called "Your Eyes", which Kenny Stowell and I wrote.

We got a gig backing up this young kid from Texas, a country crooner type guy, an ex-marine called Coogan Jones. That was his stage name, I think his real name was Craig. He was good, he had a beautiful voice, but he was kinda spaced-out. Big, good looking guy.

We ended up being the house band at the Rusty Nail. Tom McCormick's ex-wife, Edie Sing, was Coogan's manager, we pretty much had to answer to her.

Bob and I played as an acoustic duo on Thursday night, and then on Friday and Saturday, Jim and Bob and I backed up Coogan Jones. I went to bass.

Henke's nickname was Willard and I went by RJ (Robert James). RJ sounded more cowboy than "Robbie". So everybody called me RJ. So we went by RJ and Willard.

It was pretty good.

Finally, after a while Bob wanted to break away from Jones and Bob's wife, Kris, took over as manager of the band.

So Henke and I and Jim Moorehouse formed a power trio called the All Musician Orchestra or AMO, "ammo". One patron told us that's also Latin for love.

We rehearsed in Bob's living room. All over the walls of his living room were gold and platinum records from Dr. Hook.

With Bob Henke at Buffalo Rick video shoot

There was this guy who had long blonde hair and a goatee like Buffalo Bill. His name was Rick, so he was Buffalo Rick. A short guy. We did a video of a couple of his songs where we dressed up in cowboy costumes.

Kris told us that there was this girl who was looking for a band, Liza Martin. She had been working with Buffalo Rick and he had her wearing a skimpy dance hall girl outfit and I don't think she was very comfortable with that.

107

Her mother was Spanish. Not Mexican, but Spanish. And her dad was Anglo. Her name was Elizabeth Martin and for a stage name she changed it to Liza Martin (pronounced "Leeza Marteen").

So she joined the band. She was 23, 24; great voice, solid rhythm guitarist.

Liza brought along her friend, who played fiddle and mandolin and sang, Darcy DeVille – that's her real name – who was from Calgary, Alberta, Canada. She'd go back there sometimes in the summer and do coffee house gigs.

All Musician Orchestra 1985 Tempe, Arizona

So we had a five-piece band with Jim Moorehouse on drums, Bob Henke on lead guitar, Liza Martin on rhythm guitar, Darcy DeVille on fiddle and mandolin and me on bass. We had three or four part harmonies. It was just a great band.

That was probably about 1984-85.

Sometimes, when Bob wanted a bigger sound, we would use a saxophone and conga player named Ricardo Aguilar. He was a funny guy. He did one of the funniest versions of "Yakity Sax" I ever heard. He just kept getting faster and faster.

I was right in the middle of singing a song, playing bass, and he leaned over and whispered some joke in my ear. He was like that. I couldn't help but laugh.

I was doing a song by J.J. Cale called "Hey, Baby", and there's a line in there that says, "You made the day a song like I knew you would," so instead I looked right and him and sang, "You made the day a *joke*, like I knew you would,".

Liza Martin and I became a really good singing duo. We just had a connection; we could read each other's minds onstage.

Somewhere in the mid 1980's the AMO band got booked to open for BJ Thomas at a dude ranch type situation north of Scottsdale. I think they had rodeos there, too.

So I hung around backstage while Thomas did his thing. His wife, Linda, was there, real pretty, seemed like a real sweet, nice person.

The next morning, I had to fly back to Indianapolis for Christmas out of Sky Harbor airport in Phoenix.

I was walking down the passageway that goes to the plane from the gate and Linda Thomas was waiting there and she recognized me from the night before and said, "Hi!"

Pretty soon here comes BJ Thomas. He asked where I was going, and I told him I was flying to Indianapolis, because I live in a small town south of Indianapolis called Nashville.

He said, "Oh yeah, I played at the Little Nashville Opry."

We took the same flight, but different ends of the airplane. I'm sure he probably flew first class.

A really nice man. Just a little guy. Probably 125 pounds. Big voice.

That went on for a couple of years. We played at Mr. Lucky's, a big country nightclub with a huge dance floor.

109

It was a really good band, but, it was, basically, Henke had to be in charge. He just had to be, that was his personality, so we went along with it. That was AMO.

But, as things will in Phoenix, or anywhere, people dispersed and found other projects. AMO kind of scattered to the wind.

So I went to work as a bass player for a husband and wife team called Rojo and Sapphire, real names Carl and Sharon Watkins. They had nice harmonies and I harmonized and sang some lead and the drummer sang harmonies. That lasted for a year or more.

We had the house band gig in a club in Tempe that had been a girlie joint, a take-it-off type joint. I guess the owner got in legal trouble or some complaints, so he decided to get out of the girlie thing and have a band for dancing.

Carl and Sharon were nice people but I just wanted something else.

Dessert Deluxe

"Well, it helps if you're schizophrenic."

In the mid-to-late 1980's, '85 or '86, Liza was freelancing and I was kind of freelancing and we decided to start a band.

We recruited Ed Bakke on drums and Mike Ragains on lead guitar out of Rojo and Sapphire. She and I were the up-front singers for a band we called Dessert Deluxe.

It was a great band. We kicked ass.

Ed Bakke, the drummer, sang high harmonies; six foot five, 240 pounds and he sang high harmonies. A really nice guy.

The lead guitar player, Mike Ragains, had been the flat picking champion of Arizona one year. He was a really good guitar player. Also a real nice guy.

That was my favorite Arizona band. I liked AMO, AMO was slick, but there was something down-to-earth about Dessert Deluxe.

It was a really fun band and a very democratic band; no leaders. We all pretty much had an equal say-so. Whereas with AMO, Bob Henke was definitely the boss.

We had great vocals. Liza and I really locked in to each other, musically.

After years and years of working on it, I had got to where I could play bass and take harmonica solos at the same time; I could walk a bass and take a solo, not just pump it.

People would say, "How do you do that?" and I'd say, "Well, you have to be schizophrenic."

It's like when I do multi-track recordings, singing multiple parts, I say: "I'm beside myself..."

Dessert Deluxe

We played Mr. Lucky's a lot.

It was the premiere country nightclub. There were these big bass bins underneath the floor of the stage that projected out across the dance floor. There was a sound booth directly across the dance floor from the stage with a 16-track recording situation. We recorded every gig we ever did there.

I have a whole album of that stuff Dessert Deluxe did live at Mr. Lucky's. I've still got a copy of some of that somewhere that I transferred to CD. Every now and then I pull it out.

There was some really funny stage banter. Liza and I had a similar sense of humor.

She would come up with these humorous band names; "Joe Blow and the Go-Go", "Legs Akimbo and the Interceptors" or "Doris Clitoris and the Crotch Rocket"

She was funny. The crowd really liked Liza.

If anybody would shout out for song by some band we didn't know, she'd say, "We have an agreement with them; we don't do any of their songs and they don't do any of ours."

I just loved that woman.

She died in 2010, but I didn't find out until later.

We usually filled in for the house band when they got other gigs or went on vacation. Then the house band broke up and we pretty much became the house band at Mr. Lucky's in the late 1980's.

We were playing Mr. Lucky's on some Saturday afternoon when these two deejays from a big country music radio station came in with Jeff Cook from the band Alabama.

We went on break and Jeff was back stage and he asked us if we did any of his songs. We didn't do any Alabama songs, but that didn't seem to faze him.

Mike handed him his Fender telecaster and we took the stage and Mike played Liza's Ibanez.

We sang "Momma Don't Let Your Babies Grow Up to be Cowboys", stuff like that. After a few songs, the deejays jumped up there, "Lets here it for Jeff Cook, y'all be sure to come out to the show later out at...", wherever it was.

113

But Jeff didn't want to get off the stage. They had to almost drag him off the stage.

"We got to get you to the show, Jeff..."

Liza knew everybody in the music scene around Phoenix, she grew up in Levine, which is an adjoining town.

We were playing at an event called The Breeders Cup Banquet at this place called Turf Paradise, a horse track, casino and lounge near Phoenix, and the guest of honor was Tanya Tucker.

She was sitting at a table right in front of where we were playing. We started the second set with her song "Texas- (When I die)".

When Liza started singing, "When I die, I may not go to heaven..." Tanya jumped up and grabbed the microphone and started singing it herself!

She did a couple of songs with us. We did "Help Me Make It Through the Night" and "Me and Bobby McGee".

She really liked us. She said, "Let's hear it for this group!"

She looked like a million bucks, she was a tiny little thing. She had on this outfit that was red and black and had this Spanish style flat-brimmed cowboy hat.

She was a great person.

Liza got us this gig, it was a celebrity fundraiser for people with head injuries. The emcee was the actor Ben Johnson, and there were several famous folks there like Wilford Brimley and Linda Blair, James Doohan, Larry Wilcox, Lee Horsely and rodeo champ Larry Mahon, who had a line of western clothing.

And they auctioned off this memorabilia, like "Scotty" had a script from Star Trek, and so forth.

At one point, the crowd was drinking and chattering and partying and they were trying to do this auction and Wilford Brimley went up to one of the mics and said, "Now listen! We've got to get this auction done. Settle down, we'll get it done, and then we can party."

And everybody shut up and they got it done.

At some point during the afternoon, Wilford and his son got up and sang cowboy songs. And Larry Mahon was standing next to me and he turned to me and said, "Bass players are weird."

And then he just grinned and said, "You guys are great!"

After a couple of years, Dessert Deluxe faded. I freelanced some and Liza freelanced some. I sat in with other bands or did session work.

That whole Phoenix thing – I became pretty much a staple of the Phoenix music scene for several years. I was considered as good a bass player and singer as there was out there.

During that time, I hired out to do background vocal work.

We had this one session with Liza and Ron Livingston. Bob Hinke was producing a demo for some songwriter.

Ron was just a great guy. We got to be really good friends. He could play anything. He could do a lot of things.

Bob was the engineer and Liza and Ron and I did the background vocals, we did the "ahhhh's". So we were the "Wizards of Ahhhs".

We had a really good sound.

After all that stuff, Liza had gone her own way, and Ron Livingston and I started doing a thing.

Ron Privett was freelancing and he was also a booking agent, putting together a lot of throw-together bands. There were a lot of freelancers out there, including me, especially after Dessert Deluxe.

Ron Privett and I ended up doing a lot of gigs together.

Sometimes we'd do a duo, sometimes we'd do a trio. Sometimes he'd call me up and say, "RJ, I need a trio for Camelback Inn..." or someplace. "I'll give you a little extra if you'll put a trio together and provide a PA."

His dad Gene was a retired teacher and coach, and he was such a lovely man. He did all those old cowboy songs like "Tumbling Tumbleweeds" and "Back in the Saddle Again", stuff like that. Ron and Gene were originally from Arkansas.

And Kenny Scaggs, who ended up in Glen Campbell's band, he and I backed up Gene quite a bit.

Ron and I had a nice duo going. He was a good showman. He would start out "Grandfather's Clock" real slow on mandolin and then we would pick it up and do it double time. It was really neat, he was a good mandolin player.

Sometimes he would have a drummer and we would do a trio.

I worked with Merle Briganti, who was the drummer on all of those Loggins and Messina records. He moved to Scottsdale and was working with this new age lady, Sheila Ryder, who had a studio there.

Merle was a powerful drummer, almost too powerful for these smaller combos that we were doing playing these resort hotels. He was really good, but he played at concert volume – he was used to playing big rooms.

Liza and I or Ron and I would put together these trios and duos and quartets for these out-of-town convention groups coming in from Cedar Rapids or Cleveland or someplace to get out of the bad weather.

We would try to dress kind of westerny, well dressed, nice western shirts, and clean blue jeans and boots. Well groomed. Merle would show up at the gig southern California style – cutoff shorts, flip-flops, a baggy old T shirt with a flannel shirt over the top of it. He looked like a surf bum. But a nice guy. A really nice guy.

I did a couple of gigs with Jeff Dayton, who ended up being Glen Campbell's band leader.

That was the last of my operations in Arizona, and then I came back home.

I had a great experience in Phoenix. I became one of the regulars of that era in Phoenix music. I met and worked with all these great musicians and song writers and performers like Bob Henke and Tom McCormick, Don Buzard, Ron Privett, Ed Bakke and Jim Moorehouse.

Part Six:

Marriage and Fatherhood

Ohio

"It was a difficult situation…"

I had been living with Chris Smith, we'd been together six years and finally, it fell apart. So I decided to go back to Indiana.

I rented the little cottage next to the Banner Brummet cabin in Nashville. Pat Riley was living there at the time. It was owned by a guy named Judd Dahl who lived in Florida.

I moved in there in the Spring of 1989.

I ran an extra-long phone line from Pat's over to my place and we used the same number. Then we rigged a string with a bell on it, and if I answered the phone and it was for Pat, I'd ring the bell, and vice-versa.

When I was staying at the Brummet house, that's when I met Deb. She was in Ohio, but she'd come over here to see my sister.

She had gone to Ball state with Della Bridwell, who was good friends with my sister Laura, and she met those Brown County/Ball State kids through Della.

Deb told me the Brown County kids told her, "You've got to come down and see where we live." And so they did.

They pulled up at the old Ashram Restaurant about six a.m. Deb said she got out, looked around and thought, "This is home."

She grew up in Greenville, Ohio, northeast of Richmond, Indiana. It's a nice town, maybe about the size of Martinsville or Shelbyville.

So Deb got to know Laura through Della. She would come to Brown County during the summers when she wasn't teaching in Ohio. I had moved back from Phoenix.

Laura was living up on Coffey Hill. I would walk up to the post office and get her mail for her and then walk up and deliver it and sit and talk with Laura a little bit.

I was walking down these steps down to the cabin and Deb walked out. She was looking really good in those days. I had always thought that I'd like to get to know her better.

She was staying with Sue Mitchell.

I asked her to come over for drinks and dinner one night and...things led to things...

Things happened...

In August, I got a call from my sister and she said "I just got a call from Deb" and I said, "I'll guess that she's pregnant."

And she was.

It was a difficult situation, because she was separated but not divorced.

I had talked to Ron Privett a couple of times and he said, "I've got a bunch of work for you if you come back out here." So, about January of 1990, I went out to Phoenix, but Deb was still in Ohio.

Liza was living in a house her mom owned in Levine, west and south of Phoenix. She had an extra bedroom and she offered to let me stay there. I helped with the rent and helped out with the cooking when she was out gigging.

I did some gigs with Ron. I was doing some gigs, not as many as her, but making pretty good money

That lasted until May, when I got a call from Deb saying we have a daughter now. That was the Spring of 1990. So I decided I had come back here because I wanted to be with our baby.

I came back because I thought, "I need to do something about this relationship."

Deb had a year of maternity leave so she eventually made it over here a couple of months later. We came together and we got married in 1992.

She decided to go back to Ohio, because she couldn't get anything here at the kind of pay she was accustomed to. So we moved to Ohio so she could pursue her teaching career.

We stayed at her parents' summer house on Indian Lake. You know, the Cowsills were from Ohio and I think it is the Indian Lake of the pop song fame;

"...it's the scene you should make with your little ones..."

We went over there in August and the next Spring we got a house in Kenton, right in town. It was a neat old Victorian house with a nice back yard. We did a lot of work on it. For the four years we lived there, part of it was always under construction.

It had these great big picture windows in front with leaded glass bands across the top. The glass was so old it was wavy. It was a beautiful house.

In the summers when Deb was off, we'd come over to Brown County as often as we could.

When we first got to Ohio, for a year or so I didn't even look for gigs. I stayed at home and was a house dad. I was really into being dad. Erin and I went everywhere together, to the library, did the shopping. I cooked and did the laundry.

When she was a year and a half old, she had just learned to walk, and she really loved it. We'd go out walking around and she'd be making up these little three and four note melodies -

"Abee, Obee..." - she'd sing that over and over.

There's a song on my (2008) "Been Around" album called "Jack O' Lantern Moon. When Erin was about eight years old, she came up with that concept.

She and Deb were driving home, and the Harvest Moon was just rising, and she said, "Look mama, it's the Jack O Lantern moon."

And she came up with the first chorus:

"The flower blossoms disappear
"The moon is full, October's here

124

"It's the night of the Jack O Lantern moon..."

Eight years old, and she came up with that. She's working on a novel right now. She's just turned 30.

On the dining table, there were always notes, to-do lists, reminders, whatever, and if somebody would get an idea, they would go over, get a scrap of paper or a little tablet or something and write down ideas.

Erin wrote down that opening stanza for "Jack O Lantern Moon". Then Deb would come up with something and I would come up with a couple of things, I think mostly it was Deb and Erin. I made some kind of order out of them.

Then I put music to the words. I used an instrumental phrase, what they call in jazz "the head," that I had used in a song I wrote out west. And it works. It's the intro and the outro.

I would get together with a guy who I would later play in a band with, Jerry Lacher. His wife Linda and my wife were friends, they had done leaded stained glass projects together.

She left him, and I would go down about once a week and we would drink whiskey and play music. Just to take his blues away, to try to help...

We even had a couple of gigs, and we went into the studio and made a demo. But we just didn't go over.

About a year later, Deb saw an ad in the Kenton Times that said "Wanted: singing bass player for country rock trio". So I went and talked to those people and I got the job. They were called "Rowdy Country" after Hank Jr.

The wife of the band leader got me a job at the newspaper. Every Tuesday, I would go in about 4:30 in the morning and stuff newspapers into these little plastic bags.

I and the rural-route guys and the press people would stuff these different "inserts" into the regular paper – there were so many at Christmas time, you had to have a trailer behind this Chevy Suburban.

Then, I would load up this big Suburban and I would drive around to local post offices and a couple of convenience stores around Kenton, south of Toledo.

It was a nice job, a little extra money.

I was at a music store in Bellefontaine, I had bought some equipment there, and on the bulletin board was a notice for a band called the Country Rebels, they were looking for a lead player.

Keith Mathys and his wife, they were the Country Rebels and their son DJ played drums. Great folks. They're in Florida now.

I hated to leave the Sheet's (Rowdy Country) because they were really good folks, but once I met the Mathys's I just thought, "I belong with these people."

So I went over to Marion, Ohio to see the Country Rebels and talk to them and I think I sat in with them on bass. I got up and sang a couple of songs.

I played lead with them for a few rehearsals and I think I did a couple of gigs with them. But I am a very limited lead player. I do a lot of licks and passing things between chords. I know some licks and I can take solos, but I'm limited. What I do is better as a rhythm guitar player, but it's much more complicated than just strumming. I do a lot of stuff.

They seemed to tolerate me on lead...

I gave it a shot and they even hired me. But then their bass player quit after just a couple of gigs, and I told them, "You know, I'm really a bass player..."

So they hired Jerry Lacher as a lead guitar player and I went to bass. Jerry and I hit it off right away, I could tell he was a good musician.

126

We had a good sound. Jerry sang lead, Keith sang lead, I sang lead. Jerry played harmonica, I played harmonica and later on, DJ started playing harmonica on a holder while he was playing drums! For a while Sandy, Keith's wife, ran sound for us and acted as kind of a manager.

It was really good band, and we worked almost every weekend.

We had a fun sound. And Jerry was hilarious. He'd do these recitations in the middle of a song while we'd just vamp. I can't remember any of the routines now… But it was a fun band.

We played all around Ohio.

I was with a group before, I think it was before Rowdy Country, a group called Variety Pack. The leader was the drummer, and he was kind of pushy. He had gone through some Dale Carnegie course or something and he just thought he could motivate everybody "to beat the band". He just wore me out.

So, anyway, I was with the Country Rebels and we were living in a big old Victorian house there in Kenton.

Deb retired from teaching, and, eventually, she wanted to move back to Brown County, so we came over here and looked for houses.

We moved back in the summer of 1996 and she bought a house out on Christiansburg Road. Erin was six. We settled in there, and I started doing some solo stuff, like at the Brown County Inn and so on.

Deb and Erin and I were in a store across from the courthouse and we ran into Steve Miller.

He said, "Listen, I'm working with a guy named Slats Klug. We're working on a project about Brown County."

"I want you and Dave and Bob Cheevers to get in on it."

Part Seven:
Liar's Bench/
My Brown County Home

Liar's Bench

"Slats didn't know what to think about Dave and Bob and me..."

In the Fall of 1996 Steve Miller and musician Slats Klug were working on a project about Brown County inspired by the book "If You Don't Outdie Me" by Dillon Bustin.

That book was based on the journals of Frank Hohenberger, a pioneer Brown County photographer who had promoted Brown County's legend and image through the 1930's and 40's in a weekly column in the Indianapolis Star newspaper called "Down In the Hills O' Brown".

I remember Hohenberger. He was still alive when I was in high school. He died in 1963. I remember him coming out of the Bartley house, he had an apartment upstairs. He'd come out and go up the street to the Nashville House for dinner or something.

He always had the same clothes on. He had this gray felt hat, a white shirt, black suspenders, gray pants and those black ankle high shoes that old men used to wear.

Iconic Frank Hohenberger photograph "Liar's Bench"

Slats and Steve read the book and they went down to the Lilly Library and read his journals, and from there came the songs.

I think Steve's wife Ann and Slat's wife Lauren had met, and Slats and Steve got together, and Steve started telling him some of these stories about these characters of Brown County's past.

Steve said, "We're putting this thing together about Brown County." They were writing things out, and Slats had started writing some songs.

Steve wanted to use Brown County people. He knew that Dave and I had been singing together since high school. I'm sure Steve talked us all up pretty good (to Slats), Carrie Harris and Bob Cheevers and Dave Gore and me.

Slats told me after the fact, after Liars Bench was released, he said he wasn't sure about us Brown County folks at first, because he hadn't heard us.

Steve said, "I'll be giving you a call pretty soon", and not long after that, Slats got us some tapes of some of the songs he wanted us to sing.

The first demo I heard was probably "A Good Way to Die" or "My Dog Don't Lie".

Bob Cheevers was in Nashville (Tennessee) at the time. Dave was busy, I was busy, but finally, a couple of weeks later we met at Steve's office. Lauren Robert, Slats' wife at the time, stopped in, she had been in town doing something. He wanted us to sing one of his songs, but Dave and I hadn't really learned them.

I had heard of Slats. Mike Robertson (Mike's Dance Barn) had mentioned him to me. He had been in Steve Miller's (architect) office to talk about some structural issues or something and Slats had popped in looking for me.

Said he looked kind of pale, like he'd been indoors for several years...

A few weeks later, or a month, I don't know... It was winter, maybe February of 1997, I guess, we met in Steve's office and drove down outside of Unionville, where Dave Webber has his studio, Air Time Studio.

I think they had done some stuff there with Mojo Hand, the Bloomington-based zydeco and swamp rock band, but they weren't doing that so much anymore, because Slats was so involved with the Liar's Bench thing. I think they had basically broken up.

Slats didn't know what to think about Dave and Bob and me, how things were going to turn out. He was kind of apprehensive.

Once Bob and Dave and I started running through our parts and joking around and laughing it up as we always did – we were basically learning the songs on the spot – he just relaxed. He knew that we knew what we were doing.

Hell, we had been singing together for years.

They would get these outtakes of us laughing and making fun of each other and Slats and Steve would weave them into the songs.

We just went in and did the session, we did it all in about 12 hours. We probably started about noon and knocked off about midnight, I guess.

Recording "Liar's Bench"
Robbie, Steve Miller, Slats Klug

We took a break about 6:30 or 7 o'clock. Steve went down to the kitchen and made us a spaghetti dinner with salad. And we had supper and we went back to work.

I think after supper we did "My Dog Don't Lie", then we did some of those recitation, talking parts; "How much mule..." "...had to take a shoe out of it..."

134

We just did vocals. They already had most of the tracks down and his lead vocals, things like that.

Slats was good to work with. He didn't like, dominate, or anything like that. He suggested things and there were certain ways he wanted to do things and we would go along with that. But he accepted our suggestions.

We did the session, and that was it. We had no idea what they were going to do as far as mixing it, crafting the whole album. That was 1997.

Cover of "Liar's Bench" 1997

When it came out, I got a copy of "Liar's Bench" and I listened to it, and as soon as I heard it I was blown away. I thought, "Wow, this is some good shit."

And pretty soon, the word was out...

It was a hit; everybody loved it. We got great reviews in the press. We had a big write up in the Indianapolis Star, the Herald Times in Bloomington, we did a couple of radio shows. It was the talk of the town.

Steve told some stories and we did songs. It was still growing and maturing. Then, we started getting more gigs. We played at Fountain Square in Bloomington, up in the big ballroom, probably winter of 1998. We did a show at Borders Bookstore and we did one out at the Inn of the Fourwinds for the Indiana Historical Society.

We did the "Liar's Bench" show in Bloomington, Columbus, Franklin - we did a show at the Martinsville Public Library. We also did a series of Sunday matinee shows at the Nashville Follies.

We did two live "Saturday's Child" radio broadcasts at the Bloomington community radio station, WFHB, in the Firebay (WFHB is located in the old Bloomington City Hall).

The first few shows we did, I played maybe a little rhythm guitar, some percussion, you know, shakers or what not. Then Steve told Slats I was a bass player, so he said, "Let's try you on bass and see what happens."

When we were doing the bigger shows with the bigger cast, I was the bass player, period. With the smaller shows – Slats and I did a duo a lot – I played my 12-string and he'd play harmonica or accordion.

There's been nothing like the Liar's Bench/My Brown County Home projects before or since as far as I'm concerned.

Slats is brilliant. There was talk that he should've been nominated for a Grammy for Liar's Bench. It should've got one. There hasn't been anything like that music and those stories anywhere. It's an absolutely unique endeavor.

One of the reviews said something like, "Slats Klug has done for Brown County what Garrison Keillor did for Lake Wobegone, only with Brown County, it's all true."

I have to say it was one of the absolute highlights of my musical career and my life.

String Bean Reunion Show

"We took it right up to almost showtime.

It was hectic."

In November of 1997 we had the String Bean String Band reunion show.

We had about 300 people come. We got a write-up in the Ryder, or one of those Bloomington publications about the upcoming reunion concert. We had T-shirts and cassettes for sale.

We did just one show. And it took us six months to put it together, to get hold of everybody. Kenny was in California, Bob Vernon was in California, Bob Cheevers was in Nashville, Bob Lucas was in Ohio.

Bob Vernon was kind of coordinating things from LA. He was working as an assistant director on music videos, commercials, TV shows, and movies.

I think possibly it was Steve Mara who came up with the idea of a reunion. He said, you guys are coming up on 25 years. Somebody, probably me, got hold of Bob Vernon, who was our road manager and sound man and he started coordinating things and e-mailing people. We talked on the phone about things and how to get it going. I forget who exactly booked the Brown County Inn, probably Bob Vernon.

The cassette was some of these demos we had done over the years. Steve Mara and I put that together.

We took the tapes to Richard Fish at what was then Lodestone Productions, a recording studio.

He said, the way they made some of those tapes, certain brands of tape were porous, and the best way to get the moisture out of these old tapes is to bake them at a low temperature.

So he baked them.

He re-mastered them on Digital Audio Tape. But somehow, in the process, they became unplayable.

We sent off and had 200 cassettes made.

Reunion show

Jim Tracy did the art work and had the J-card, they called it, that went inside the cassette, manufactured. He was working for a T-shirt company in Bloomington. Alan Jones did one page of it and I pretty much wrote the liner notes and compiled the list of players of each song from memory. Steve Mara put up most of the money to have the cassettes manufactured.

We had 200 copies made and we sold them at the reunion concert. We pretty much sold out. Sold some of them, gave some of them away. The sale of those tapes paid for the PA and engineer.

I have two or three copies on CD now. Thirteen songs.

Town Hall was partitioned in two for a wedding and these couples went way, way over, so we couldn't do a sound check. While the PA guys were getting set up, we were picking out songs, making a set list, that afternoon. We took it right up to almost showtime. It was hectic.

We hired a big fancy PA for the show. Our former manager Alan Deck emceed and Frank Jones opened up the show.

It was recorded, but when we did this reunion show, and this happens, it was a reason to gather, a lot of people who didn't normally go out would show up to see us guys. But a bunch of them ended up talking through the whole show.

Chris Bryan and a guy named Scott Davis did the sound and lights

It was a party.

Dave might still have a recording of it. I think Alan was recording as well.

My Brown County Home

"Pink Roses and Wine"

The second Brown County themed album, "My Brown County Home" is the next year, I suppose, 1998-99.

After the first record, Steve and Slats had a falling out.

Slats wanted to do a follow-up soon after the first year, to make some money and keep people interested in us.

Steve was still part of the live shows, he was the Storyteller. His early vision of the show was it would be a story teller with songs.

Slats was starting to think that I was fairly valuable to him, as far as creativity goes. I did a lot of research on some of those characters, wrote out some stuff for him and some of the stuff we used on the radio shows we did.

Slats wanted to get going, "Let's get this thing going! Let's do it! We've got some momentum going!"

Steve and Slats just had different ideas about things, and Slats decided to go ahead and break away. I think Steve took it philosophically.

He still had a solo gig once in a while where he would tell stories about Brown County, which is what he did in the early days of the project. Steve is a great storyteller.

Sometime shortly after that, just a few days later, I think, Slats and I had lunch. He said, "I'm going to go ahead. I'm going to change some of the lyrics to these songs."

He said, "What do you think about this? I'll just handwrite a contract between the two of us, and you'll be my partner on this next album and help me with the live shows."

I said, "Sure!"

I kind of became his executive officer and right hand man. He depended on me for a lot; emceeing and that kind of thing.

We did the "My Brown County Home" album, which I think is my favorite.

Slats had written this song about the relationship between V.J. Cariani and Marie Goth which he called "Pink Roses and Wine". He played it for me and I said, "I want to do that song. I'll do the VJ Cariani part and I know just the person to do the Marie Goth part."

Liza Martin was living in Nashville (Tennessee) singing on demos and so on, getting into homeopathic medicine, things like that.

A lot of the Phoenix folks ended up in Nashville. She was married to Matt McKenzie, a Scottsdale boy who was Don Williams' bass player. He had been in the house band at Mr. Lucky's. A fine bass player and a really nice guy.

He'd been with Lyle Lovett for a while, and Patty Loveless. He was then playing with Don Williams, who according to him, was just this good old boy, unaffected by his stardom.

So I was there at Slats' house and he called Liza and she said, "Yeah, I'll do it!"

On June 19 Don Williams was playing at the Little Nashville Opry, so Matt was on the road in Nashville, Indiana.

Liza drove up from Nashville to Slats' house and we went over to Air Time Studio outside Unionville and we did "Pink Roses and Wine".

"My Brown County Home" 1999

Then, Slats had her sing the alto part on "Soft and Low" about the Bohalls and the basket weaving – there were no boys to take over, so Irene, one of the daughters, was taught to weave baskets, and a woman had never been taught those things.

And she sang a part on "Blood Alley Women" as well. So it was a very productive session.

She met up with Matt that night, he was at the BCI, and they came out to see Deb and Erin and I, I guess at that point we were still out on Christiansburg Road.

We went into town to the Art Gallery. She wanted to buy a couple of paintings. They had just had the Hoosier Heritage Art show, but they had taken down all the paintings and had not rehung their regular collection.

So we walked up to June Bryant's next to the Post Office and Liza bought a couple of June's paintings.

I wanted her to meet Dave, I had talked so much about him and we used to do "OD'd on Love" which was a song he wrote. Really clever.

When I kissed her last night I was near Nirvana
I was seeing pure light doves
I'll have to drop a lot of downers just to get myself straight cause
I almost OD'd on love..."

She met Dave and we took a couple of pictures.

When My Brown County Home was ready, Slats asked me to write the liner notes. He edited them, but Deb, my wife at the time, she and I wrote the liner notes.

I tell you, once your creative juices get to flowing, it's like you can't stop it. I got on a roll. I was writing stuff right and left.

We lived down on Christiansburg Road. There was a pole barn structure behind the house, part of it was a studio that had been built by Mike Scoville, who was an artist for Leaning Tree Cards. He lived out there for a few years.

I spent a lot of time out there, writing and practicing or what not.

I stepped out one June evening and the whippoorwills were just jamming. There were four of them; one to the east, one

144

to the north one to the south and one to the west, singing back and forth to each other.

I heard that, and pow! it hit me -

"Half-moon in a starry sky,"
"Whippoorwills calling back and forth,
"Time for dreams in Peaceful Valley..."

It just came to me.

It eventually went with the song, "Peaceful Valley" as liner notes.

The last line in the song is female voices singing,

"Time now for dreams..."

So, I had a lot to do with "My Brown County Home" and that's my favorite of those Brown County records, and Slats agreed with me on that.

Slats worked really hard on that, he really cranked.

He came out to the house on Christiansburg Road to look at a couple of paintings Deb had, a Carl Graf and an E.K. Williams. I could see he was tired, he was sleep deprived, cranking this thing out.

Finally, he found a painting by Curry Bohm and that's what he used for the cover of My Brown County Home.

I found a couple of Hohenberger photographs at the library, and I said, "Here's the picture you need to use on 'Natural Law' about the moonshiner." Tom Rosnowski and John Franz sing it. John was Oliver, the game warden

The picture, it's down at the library, he's sitting on a stump or something and there's a still there and he's got a rifle across his arm and he's looking really mean. Like, "I'm gonna get your ass."

I said, "Slats you've gotta see this picture, its perfect for 'Natural Law'." When he saw it he said, "Oh, yeah, that's it."

When it came out in 1998, My Brown County Home was well received.

We did big shows in Town Hall at the Brown County Inn. We did nine holiday shows starting the Saturday after Thanksgiving and three or maybe four concerts for Big Brothers/ Big Sisters with a full cast.

We did it at the Brown County Playhouse, a couple of times at the Seasons Convention Center, and we did one show at the high school auditorium, that was one where I was in charge.

Slats was tired. He would get really tensed up before these big shows because he was so afraid something would go wrong, but nothing ever did. We nailed it every time.

We were so jacked up on adrenaline, as soon as we would take the stage - the applause – it was really uplifting. It made you step up a level or two and really do your best.

Dave and Robbie at one of the live shows

Longshot

"...And his wife said,
"Well, that's a long shot..."

In that same era as the Liar's Bench/My Brown County Home projects, probably around 2000, I was in a band called Longshot.

I was in the house band at Mike's Dance Barn, playing rhythm guitar, second guitar, harmonica, and I sang. It was a nice steady gig but Mike didn't pay that much. If I had something to do with Slats, I had to beg off and I wouldn't be there. They got along without me.

Rick Gilles, a construction guy who was originally from Shelbyville but had been here for several years, came in one night to Mike's and somehow the subject of him needing a bass player came up.

So I left Mike to go with Rick's band Dixie Drive, I was the bass player and sang. He had this kid Tony on guitar, and Jim Rawlins on drums. Then Tony left the band and he got Kenny Strong on guitar and we hit it off; he liked the way I played bass and I loved his guitar playing.

While I was doing that "Pink Roses and Wine" session with Liza, Dixie Drive had a gig at the Eagles in Greensburg, a good bunch of folks. Larry Morely, a musical fixture in Bloomington for years that I had worked with in the past, took my place on bass in Dixie Drive for just that night.

During that night, I'm not sure how, Rick got to drinking quite a bit – he liked his white Russians – and he started complaining to Jim about dragging the beat, and I wouldn't doubt that Larry had a buzz and *he* was dragging and Jim couldn't compensate or whatever. And Rick got in Jim's face and they almost came to blows. But Rick was always so nice to me.

Of course, I heard about all this after-the-fact.

So, Jim and Kenny decided to leave Rick. Kenny called me and told me what was going on and basically, Jim and Kenny and I decided to form a trio.

And Jim was telling his wife about it and she said, "Well that's a long shot..." That's where the name came from.

We used Slats sometimes, when he was available, on keyboard and accordion and harmonica, vocals. Slats couldn't commit to a bar band too much. We still had four "Brown County" CD's to go, he had a mountain of work in front of him, and we were putting on these lives shows as well.

Jim, or maybe Kenny, or both of them knew this woman from Shoals, Indiana, named Carla Sims. I had played with her husband, Gary, who was a bass player, back in the 80's with a guy named Bob Jones, who was a Bloomington musical fixture, a real character.

He (Jones) knew "G" "E minor" "C" and "D", and that was about it. Even if we were playing in "F", he would play in "G". We would just turn his guitar off. But he was a really good mandolin player, and played a rudimentary fiddle.

He was a real character. He said "Yo!" a lot.

We connected with Carla and she worked out well, good singer, nice lady. She even did a live "Slats Klug and Friends" show at Town Hall (BCI). I think it was a Valentine's Day show we did one year.

But, her unwed daughter had a baby and was living with her and Gary, and that drive from Shoals to Bloomington, that's a haul. When I was with Dixie Drive, and Longshot, we'd play at the Eagles in Shoals, so I know.

So Carla dropped out of the band, she had a lot on her plate, and we got Carolyn Dutton for a while, she was in and out. And then Jim mentioned Stephanie Walker – it was Scrougham at the time.

Stephanie had just left this band in Martinsville, and she was available. I had heard about her, and I'm pretty sure she had heard about me. So she came to the studio where we rehearsed to sit in, as kind of an informal audition.

As soon as I met her I knew that something was going to happen between us. We started singing together and it was good, real good.

So she joined the band and we took off and we played all over the place; Columbus, Greensburg, Martinsville, Bloomington, Indy, Spencer, Shoals, Bedford, you name it. We played American Legion halls, Eagles, Elks, various bars.

Carolyn was in and out of the band, Slats a little bit. The core of it was Kenny, Jim, Stephanie and I. That was a lean, mean machine. That was a wicked band.

Stephanie is one of my favorite singers in the whole world. Our voices just blended together so well.

I've sung with a lot of women and all of them were good; Beth Lodge Rigal and Lauren Robert, of course. But Liza Martin and Stephanie Walker, I've just got this thing with them on stage, we could just read each other's minds. We'd say the same thing at the same time, that kind of stuff. We had this rapport.

We were good friends.

Kenny Strong is just a wicked, wicked guitar player. Really good. One of the best I've ever worked with – him and Bob Henke. Jack Bessire's up there with them, too. And Jeff Foster, of course. And Kenny Stowell.

We did classic country, classic rock - all covers. We had three-part harmonies with Stephanie and me and Jim singing harmonies and lead on a couple of songs, like "Gimme Three Steps".

We did everything from Patsy Cline's "Crazy" to things like a "Twist and Shout/Hang on Sloopy" medley, and everything in between. Kenny did a great guitar version of Floyd Cramer's piano instrumental "Last Date". We did "Tequila", which had been a hit for "The Champs". Kenny was great.

The Champs was a bunch of studio musicians, and when they had that hit, they had to put together a band to go out and tour, and guess who was in that band? Glen Campbell *and* Seals and Crofts. Before any of them had become stars.

We did "Georgia on My Mind", "Mustang Sally", stuff like that. It was a great band, it really was. We were together for about five years.

We did a five or six song demo but we hardly ever used it.

Glen Campbell was playing out at the Little Nashville Opry maybe about 2004-05, and we were playing in the bar at the BCI on a Friday night, "The Corncrib Lounge", or as Bob Cheevers calls it, the cornhole lounge.

Live Entertainment in the
Corn Crib Lounge
REVIVAL
Friday and Saturday Nights 9:00-1:00

HAPPY HOUR PRICES
EVERY DAY 11am to 7pm

And there was Kenny and Russell Scaggs, these brothers I had worked with out in Arizona, and the drummer from the Mr. Lucky's house band. They had since become part of Glen Campbell's organization.

So we said "Hi!" and we were talking and with them was this tall, incredibly well-built young lady in tight jeans and boots and a western shirt. She was hot. What a body!

So Kenny says, "Hey this lady is Debbie and do you think she could do a song with you guys?"

I said, "Sure, what do you want to do?"

And she said, "How about Georgia on My Mind?"

I said, "I do it in F."

She said, "That's the key I do it in!"

She got up and did a great job.

And I found out later she was Glen Campbell's daughter. She was part of his show, doing backing vocals.

Late the next night, Saturday, there were probably only about five or six people left in the place. You could hear the diesel bus engine from the bar, because the Campbell organization was staying at the BCI.

Russell Scaggs came in, "RJ how are you doing?"

He said, "Were heading up to Wisconsin."

Jeff Dayton walks in, "RJ, how ya doin?, I see you've still got that same old black bass."

"Yup. You want to do a number or two?"

So Kenney handed him his guitar. Jeff's a really good guitar player. We did some classic country rock things and he took the solo.

Then they were gone, off to Wisconsin.

Slats Klug and Saint Blue Cloud

More Brown County records and shows

We just kept plugging away, making more recordings. I usually refer to the whole series as the Liar's Bench/ My Brown County Home series.

From the Liars Bench in 1997 to 2007, it was just about a ten year run with six albums and heaven knows how many shows.

After My Brown County Home, we did the first Christmas album "A Brown County Christmas". That was Slats' idea.

Then the next year, we did the second Christmas album. Then "Lies and Love Songs", and the last one was "Sweet Magnolia". All in the course of about ten years.

I thought that was a pretty good run. That was a lot of artistic fulfillment for me. That put me over the top.

I'm not trying to brag, but I have been called a legend. In Brown County, anyway. I'm a big fish in a small pond, and that's ok.

That's what Slats ended up doing. He finally got over trying to chase the big deal in New York and then Chicago.

The whole experience was demanding and exhilarating. It was a hoot. We worked hard.

"Lies & Lovesongs" 2003

We'd get together with nine, ten, eleven people at these rehearsals for our big shows, the holiday shows, and the ones for Big Brothers/Big Sisters. We'd rehearse in Slat's living room.

The original Air Time Studio was in the upstairs of an old house that Dave Webber lived in. A couple of years later he started building a new facility attached to the house.

Between Slats and Dave Webber, they came up with some really nice sound effects and things like that, so it wasn't just songs. He'd slip in little segments of us laughing or talking after a song. Webber recorded everything.

154

Sounds like horse hoofs and sleigh bells were pre-taped "in the wild" and added to the mix.

The players would vary once in a while, but the core was Slats, Lauren, Doug Harden, Dave Gore, Beth Lodge Rigal and Mike Moody on drums, Kenny Strong on guitar and myself on bass.

Cast of one of the holiday shows

And we had smaller versions, Slats and I, or Slats and I with Lauren and Dave.

John Franz had been singing on the street corner in Nashville before Slats put him on the Liar's Bench record. I think he ended up being on all the records we did except for maybe Sweet Magnolia.

We did those Christmas albums in the summer time, so they'd be ready for Christmas.

We did "Have Yourself a Merry Little Christmas" and it's Beth singing the melody with Lauren doing the harmonies. But in the live holiday shows, I sang the melody and the girls sang the harmonies and we all sang a capella.

155

It was just too good. I love singing with women. Like with Liza Martin, we had a really good vocal thing going.

It's the vocals that makes those records as much as anything.

Carolyn Dutton was on the first Christmas record. Brent Smith, a guy from Cincinnati, played dobro and banjo. We used Brian Lapin for a couple of the live shows. He and Doug Hardin had the Not Too Bad Bluegrass Band.

"Sweet Magnolia" 2004

Deb, Erin and I moved up on Bryson Lane, across from the north park entrance, up above where old 46 and new 46 meet, into the old Onya LaTour place, Saint Blue Cloud, she called it.

The building right down below was her studio and she lived there for a while. She lived very simply.

She was a neat lady. She was bohemian before anybody knew what bohemian was. Peasant skirts, peasant blouses, turquoise jewelry. She went to Russia in the 1930's.

She was living in a house in Bloomington and my dad and I painted it high-gloss, bright, barn red with white trim. She gave me some beads. I wore those for quite some time, then... lost in the shuffle...

Jim Brennemar was CEO of the Community Foundation, and the office manager was a girlfriend of mine. Jim wanted to do a little afternoon music festival as an awareness builder for the Foundation.

So Slats put a quartet together of Slats, Lauren and Dave and me. Some covers, too. The set was probably 20 minutes or half an hour.

A guy came up to me after our set and said, "Now I like Bluegrass, but that's all I've been hearing all day except you guys. It was a nice change of pace. They need to get more guys like you."

With Dave at Christmas Show

That last big Big Brothers/Big Sisters show we did, Slats didn't want to do it. He'd get really nervous. He was always very apprehensive whether we would flub up – which we never did – we never did mess up, no clunkers that I ever heard, no train wrecks, not even close.

But Slats had to carry a heavy load. I can see why he turned the show over to me. I was honored that he had that much confidence in me.

He didn't want to do it so he said, "Do you want to do this show?" So I said, "OK." So I got Erin, who was maybe ten or eleven years old, she sang Molly's song from Liar's Bench and "We Live Within These Hills" with the whole ensemble.

When we were doing the bigger shows with the bigger cast, I was the bass player, period. With the smaller shows – Slats and I did a duo a lot – I played my 12-string and he'd play harmonica or accordion.

We'd be doing stuff from Liar's Bench, My Brown County Home and other things, a Roger Miller tune here, Stuff like "Battle of New Orleans," some classic country things, a folk song or two. It was a good act.

A real good act. Sometimes Dave would join us, or Lauren and Dave or just Lauren.

Part Eight:
A Troubadour's Life

MoodyKlug'n'Bowden

The Fish Fry Band

Besides Longshot, I was really busy doing Slats Klug stuff, plus my solo stuff; I was really busy. There was a period there when I had six gigs in five days. And another time I had four gigs in three days. That was the early 2000's.

Longshot rehearsed all the way over on the far east end of Columbus and we played all over the southern part of the state. So we carpooled, Stephanie came and picked me up.

And one day we were going to, I think, Seymour, and we were driving along and I said,

"You know, I lost my sister in 1990."

She said, "I know."

I said, "Would you be my sister?"

She said, "Sure!"

And so Stephanie's my sister, in spirit and song. I call her Sis. And we are tight as ticks. We always call each other on our birthdays and at Christmas time.

Longshot ended up getting this keyboard player who was originally from Seymour - we played the Eagles and the American Legion in Seymour. Kenny wanted to add another instrument because he was the only guitar player.

The guy that booked us at the Legion gave us the number for a guy named Michael Henderson who, in high school, had been in a band with John Mellencamp. So Michael joined the band. He had a couple of electronic keyboards and sang lead vocals as well, he really added a lot to the band.

But I knew early on that he was fixin' to be the boss of the band. Before that, we were a democratic band, we really were; nobody was in charge, a really mutual feeling.

But it was fun. We had a great sound.

Michael was throwing a lot of current country hits at us to learn, and I was so busy with all this other stuff I didn't really have a chance to work hard on those songs Michael was pitching.

I showed up at rehearsal one time and I didn't have this one Lynyrd Skynyrd song "Red White and Blue", and he got upset. At this point, he was thinking it was his band, he was the boss.

He had been with a band before us that had broken up, and I came to think that he had probably caused the breakup. Otherwise, a good guy. He just didn't fit the mold of the band. He was kind of the odd man out.

So instead of having rehearsal, he called a meeting. And he said because I hadn't gotten the material down yet, he was "offended". Not upset, not hurt, not disappointed, "offended". That pissed me off.

I kept my cool, but you probably could tell.

I said, "Well, I've got so much going on right now, I may not be able to stay in the band, I'll call you in a couple of days and let you know." And Stephanie, who can read me like a book, came up to me on the side and said, "Don't forget me" because she knew already I was gone.

I had pretty much made up my mind then and there, but I was going to think on it a while. So I did. Then I called them up and said, "I'm gone"

That would've been around 2005, 2006.

So I just kind of free lanced for a while.

Slats and I started a trio with Mike Moody, who was playing drums in some of those big shows we did.

The first set would be me on my 12-string, Slats on accordion and harmonica and Moody on drums, no bass. And we would do more acoustic oriented stuff. And some things from the CD's like "My Dog Don't Lie".

Then Slats would move over to electronic keyboard and I would move to bass and we'd start rocking. It was a really good trio.

163

We called it MoodyKlug'n'Bowden, and we would say, "It's like Farfegnugan" - that Volkswagen ad was out around that time.

I really enjoyed that band, it was fun. We got people dancing. That was a great group.

Moody is one of my all-time favorite drummers to work with. He's just great. And a really nice guy.

I remember seeing him way back in high school in Columbus. After the (basketball) sectionals, there was a dance at the Donner Center and he was in a group called the XL's. They were just kids. But I thought even then he was good. Of all the guys in the band, he most impressed me, and he's been doing it ever since.

At The Fig Tree in Helmsburg

One New Year's Eve, probably around 2005, Loretta Gooden was in Town Hall at the BCI and we were in the lounge.

She was a really good singer, but she tended to want to sing too many ballads. She was playing all these ballads and people wanted to boogie, it was New Year's Eve! So a bunch of them spilled over into the lounge, where we were playing danceable music.

That was a great night!

Stephanie and I decided we could do a duo.

So for a couple of years we played the winery and some other things here and there. She had a connection with the Masonic Home in Franklin and we'd do Christmas banquets, that kind of thing, for the folks there. It's a retirement home.

Dave, Stephanie and Rob – "The Vocal Yokels"

And that came off really well for a couple of years and that was really fun. 2010 to 2012, somewhere in that area.

I also played bass and sang for several gigs with the Reel Tyme String Band which was Danny Hardin, Rick Hedrick, Brandon Lee (a whiz kid) and Chris Bryan.

Now, as the years moved on, as they do so fast anymore, Slats would put together these throw-together bands; me, Mike

Moody or Jim Rawlins on drums, Lauren, Ken Strong on guitar. It was the Slats Klug Band at one time. It was the Fish Fry Band.

We played mostly in Bloomington. We did a thing down outside of Mitchell. It was some kind of New Age tree-hugging thing. There were some Native Americans there doing drumming and chanting. We did a couple of sets.

My latest project, released in 2008, is my solo album "Been Around".

I'm really proud of it.

I've wanted to do that for years and I finally got it together after years of working on it.

"Been Around" 2008

I saw what Slats Klug was doing with his Rebo Publishing Company, so I decided to do the same. I got some financial backing and I did the album. My Publishing Company is "Moonsongs Publishing". I have four instrumentals that I wrote out west called Moonsongs I, II, III, and IV.

"Been Around" isn't all my stuff, but it's all original. There are collaborations with my ex-wife, Deb, and even my daughter, Erin.

Deb gets a lot of co-writing credits on it. She was an English teacher. She's now a published author of many books. She would come to me with these lyrics like, "What Would You Do?" is one of the best things we ever did. The music came really fast for that.

On "High Lonesome Wind", she has credit for the two verses, she re-worded them to make them work a lot better than what I had. The chorus is all my words, and my music.

Slats is on there, as are Erin, Dave Gore, Jim Moore, Jim Rawlins, Carolyn Dutton and Doug Hardin.

Other than one track, I did all the bass and I did all the rhythm guitars. On one song Scot Merry played bass and Jim Moore played a guitar track along with me. We did that in Nashville, Tennessee and then I later added Slats on accordion and Doug Harden on mandolin.

On the song "Faraway", I did all three harmony parts. On "High Lonesome Wind" I sang a second part. I was beside myself.

I'm proud of it. The best compliment I got, probably the highest praise, was from Slats. I sent him a copy, of course, he played on it, and he said, "I think song for song, it's a really good album."

I thought, that's a high compliment, because he's very discerning and very particular. If Slats Klug likes it, I've got it made in the shade.

Part Nine:

Home Again to Stay

After the show is over…

Regrets, lessons learned, and good advice

I've had a good life, crazy as it is.

I can't believe I've lived this life, played with all these people.

So far, so good…

Like anyone, I have some regrets. I've made mistakes, but I've done a lot, learned a lot.

Have you ever seen that movie, "Dangerous Heart" with Jeff Bridges?

He's an over-the-hill country singer and a hard core alcoholic. But he turns himself around toward the end. He loses a young lady who adored him but couldn't deal with his drinking. Trying to deal with his failed career.

There's a lot of truth in that film.

171

I lost a couple of dear relationships with women because of the music. It took all my time or it took my affections away. I couldn't commit, I was on the road, wasn't home that much. So I lost a couple of real dear relationships. For the most part I've remained friends with those women, but I still get a pang once in a while if I run into them.

I did think about giving up the music career for a short time back in the 1970's to pursue a relationship with a woman, but I had to get back into it. I just had to do it. I was compelled.

I have to say this: the deterioration of my marriage led to the alienation of my daughter, and she still doesn't want anything to do with me. So, that's definitely a regret.

And a lot of that had to do with my drinking. It got worse and worse and it got to the point where I was basically worthless, musically.

I'm sure it probably caused me to fail at a few things. Maybe I could have got more accomplished as far as a record deal or getting songs published. But I got my fulfillment on that with the Liar's Bench/My Brown County Home run.

At this point I don't regret having pursued the music. The failures of some of the side relationships, I regret that. As far as trying to be as good as I could be, to go as far as I could go in the business, I don't regret that at all.

It was worth it to be considered an equal by people like Slats Klug and Bob Henke, Paul Spradlin, Jeff Dayton and Tom McCormick, these people. That was something that I have always been proud of.

One of the highlights of my musical career was that these incredible players considered me an equal. That's incredible.

Tom McCormick, who wrote the opening song on Been Around, "Alive and Pickin'", wrote this one called "Sadie" about his ex-wife:

"Sadie, it's been raining for a week now,
"The change is nice, but it sure can bring you down,
"Been thinking about the old days and how strange it is
"Not having you around,
"You played me like a game of Solitaire,
"I was losing one card at a time,
"Sometimes I hear you laughing in the sunshine,
"Sadie lady you've been on my mind."

I love his lyrics.

I talked to him on the phone out in Arizona a couple of years ago. He's got emphysema – forty years of smoking Marlboros – that was the end of his singing career.

It was just an amazing experience, all through the years. It was an interesting time to be in the business.

It started with the beginning of the Beatles in America, the Stones, the Doors, the Animals, the Beach Boys. Jimi Hendrix. Now, rock'n'roll has advanced so much, it's gone in so many different directions, some I don't care for.

The "suits" in the music industry, when they see something that comes up strong, they want to milk it till its dry. Until people get sick of it. Then something else will come along and they'll go for that.

I read this interview with Bob Seeger in Rolling Stone back in the 70's. They call Bruce Springsteen "The Boss", but I think Bob Seeger was the boss. He had such a pure approach to things.

He was asked for advice for those starting out.

He said, "Listen to the pioneers of rock'n'roll, like Chuck Berry and Bo Didley, Big Joe Turner, Buddy Holly, Jerry Lee Lewis.

I guess, just learn the basics. Listen to the pioneers and learn the basics and then you can kind of go wherever you want to go.

I have noticed in the last ten years or so there are a lot of young players who are going for the basics, going for classic styles, people like Keenan Rainwater.

You've got to get out there and pursue a career, mix and mingle. I spent a year in California, years in Arizona, years on and off the road.

You have to be able to get along with people.

I ran into a guy out there in Arizona who was a pretty good talent, but he was obnoxiously cocky. I just couldn't stand the guy. Luckily, I only did one gig with him.

You've got to get out there.

I spent all that time in Arizona and worked with some great people. Of course, we were on the road for four years with String Bean String Band.

One night you might be in the LSU auditorium opening up for Vanilla Fudge or in some club opening up for Jimmy Page and the Yardbirds, and then within a couple of weeks be playing in Breckinridge, Minnesota, out in the middle of nowhere playing for six or eight people who could give a damn one way or another about what you've got to say.

Alan Deck, who was our manager in those early years of String Bean, he got us on that supper club circuit, we were having a meeting one day and he said,

"You guys are riding high right now, doing the supper club circuit and getting write-ups in the local entertainment press, playing Butler University and all that stuff, but one day you guys are going to bomb."

And we sure did. More than once.

It covers the whole spectrum, from down and dirty in Breckinridge or at No Dogs Allowed to playing a concert club in Evanston, Illinois with Vasser Clemens and doing bluegrass festivals on the East coast, playing with well-known people of the genre.

Being on the same stage and in the same show as the Dirt Band and John Hartford, Roger McGuinn and BJ Thomas, and on and on and on.

It's been a hoot!

Back Home…

"So many roads I have seen,
"Changing days and different lives"

Now, I'm kind of in semi-retirement. I do the winery and maybe an occasional party.

I play at the winery fairly often. Sometimes I play private parties here and there. We have the Sunday jam, that's been going on more than a year now. We sit in a circle and swap songs. Those jams are a lot of fun.

Carolyn Dutton and I were booked at the winery last weekend. A couple of weeks ago, Carolyn had fallen and injured her shoulder and she couldn't make the date, so I called Stephanie.

She called back and said she had this little band, could she bring them along? Stephanie Walker/Cooper and I are the "Vocal Yokels" and this other band was "Blue Eyes, Gray Skies."

It was a hoot – three part harmonies, mandolin, harmonica and Stephanie and I. Then in the middle of the night, I left the stage and Stephanie's band did some of their show.

One of the ladies who worked at the winery said it was the best show she had seen there. Everybody loved it, and we made 92 bucks in tips.

One time Stephanie and I, when we had our duo, got $149 in tips. That's on top of our pay of $100 each. One lady said, "I don't even like country music, but you guys, we really enjoyed it."

The record was last Summer or Spring (2019), Carolyn and I did our duo there and we made $199 in tips.

When Carolyn takes a solo, the crowd just whoops and hollers. Because she is so dynamic. "Sixteen Tons" or "Ain't no Sunshine", she just tears it up. Both of those songs are in A minor, which is a really passionate key as far as I'm concerned.

We have a whole group of regulars who come in to see us, and they're very excited about the live music. When you're getting that good feedback from the crowd, it lifts you up another couple of levels.

It's a high. It's a real, genuine high.

I'm still writing songs and I guess I haven't completely ruled out making another record. I don't know. I have the material.

At this point, I've been in a studio so much over the years. I did a lot of session work out in Arizona, vocals, guitar, harmonica, and I was known more as a bass player out there, although I had a lot of guitar gigs too.

I have a song, it took me seven years to get this thing right. I had the basic idea, the germ of it. I went through key changes and all kinds of stuff, re-did the lyrics, it's called "Sweet Young Song".

It's about growing up in Brown County.

"Running down to the cool green water in the hot July summertime,
"Swimming for a while, fishing too in the shade, out of the sunshine,
"Those summer days, that sweet young song,
"Rolling Through my mind..."

"Way back when is in my memory
"Pictures in my older mind,
"In my dreams I go a wandering,
"Hoping to find
"Those Summer days, that sweet young song,
"Rolling through my mind.

"Troubled times they come and go,
"So many roads I have seen,
"Changing days and different lives,
"Right now I'm living in between."

It's up tempo and it's got quick chord changes.

I used to go for as many chords as I could, but now I'm in this minimalist mode. And I think sometimes the melodies become more complicated because the chord patterns are so simple. It's interesting.

Music is a puzzle to be figured out. And I'm not generally a puzzle person. Even the lyrics are a puzzle to me. You've got to find a rhyming scheme, say the things you meant to say. I write free verse, prose poetry, too.

You have to think it through.

Sometimes the muse comes fast.

Erin's song, that came to me in about 20 minutes and it was done. I was standing in the dining area at the Onya Latour house, looking out on the sloping yard.

She came walking around the corner of the deck with her Walkman headphones on and sat on her swing. And this song just came to me. And luckily, I was standing in front of the dining room table, where the notes and things were. Deb was always writing things down, I was always writing things down.

And it just came to me – melody, words, everything. I couldn't keep up. The muse was kicking my ass.

It's a high like I've never had except for maybe really good sex. It's like the endorphins or whatever go Pow! A natural high.

At the Sunday afternoon jam

It looks like my Terre Haute friend Karen and I have this songwriting thing going, which is good.

She's been kind of keeping back in the corner, musically, but she's got a pretty singing voice. She finally got a singing gig doing background vocals for this guy in Terre Haute who's putting together an album.

I wrote this song for her, "My Forever Brand New Friend", which I recorded and gave her a copy of. It's a love song, basically. From a soul mate to a soul mate. She's a real, true friend.

I think it's one of my better songs, at least from this period of my creative life.

I've played it out a couple of times and it turns out, women seem to really like that song. I told Frank (Jones) that one day and he said, "Women really like songs about women". A typical Frank Jones comment.

Karen handed me a sheet of lyrics, a couple of stanzas that could easily be a song. I took the lines and put a rhyming scheme to them and put some music to them. It's about "Springtime is comin', she's comin' for you."

"If women would sit on a bench made for liars,
"They'd tell you a story about a woman from elsewhere
"As winter was dying and Spring came anew
"Springtime's a comin, she's comin for you.
"Come on young green grass and dandelion flowers,
"Lilacs and bees dance in sunshine for hours,
"They whisper sweet nothings when they come back around,
"In the dew covered morning you'll hear the sweet sound.
"In spring you will find her as you're drawing near,
"Please tell me my fortune I so need to hear,
"She'll stare like you're crazy and then say with a smile:
"The season is changing, it's magic, my child!
"Roaming through woods looking for mushrooms,
"She'd leave one behind, so they'd come back again,
"She's comin' for you,
"Springtime's comin' my friend."

It's got a peppy 6/8 beat, an Irish folk song sound to it. Anyway, I've been working on that for the past few days.

At Christmas, we wrote a Christmas song! She came up with the words and half a melody and I figured out the chords and put some music to the chorus.

We have a good time together.

181

Sometimes I play private parties here and there. Not necessarily for money, but usually they give me money anyway. Not always a bunch, but it doesn't matter because I get to eat for free and visit with all these great Brown County People.

John Sisson coined the term years ago, we're "Hill Apes".

It's coming on to nine years that I've been back here on a permanent basis and I love it. This is my home. I'm a Brown Countian.

For the most part, I get the feeling that people here know who I am, respect my journey, respect my craft.

I'll be with somebody who grew up someplace else but now lives here, at the post office or the drugstore or the grocery store, and all these people say "Hi", and these transplant people will say, "You know everybody!"

I know this town and this county upside down. I know all these people I grew up with and all of these people I got to know in my adulthood.

The people are great.

It's a lovely place.

Afterword

A note from the ghost...

That's me in 1972

If you're like me, born at the tail end of the baby boom with older siblings, your taste and experience of popular music is probably dependent upon them. Whether because they introduced you to certain musicians and bands or types of music, or because you rebelled against the kind of music they liked.

I grew up in rural southern Indiana, in a small wooded county with one major town, a little village, really, of about 500 folks called Nashville. We never even went to Nashville very much until we reached high school age (that's where the county's only high school was located).

I wasn't very old, probably far enough along that my older siblings were in high school and I was just to the age of contemplating making the big jump to "town" – the high school at that time was grades seven through 12 – when my next oldest brother told me about the then burgeoning local rock'n'roll scene.

185

In every little town across America, kids were picking up guitars, drums, and keyboards and following the siren call of rock'n'roll.

And I can still recall a conversation where my brother told me about Robbie Bowden. Robbie was a "town kid" – he had had the privilege of growing up in town (tiny Nashville), around lots of other kids, unlike our experience of pretty much growing up with each other out in the woods.

My brother had seen Robbie play with one of his early bands, called the "East/West Wire Service", and he was impressed.

"If anybody from here ever makes it in rock'n'roll, it will be him," my brother predicted knowingly.

I always took that as an article of faith. I guess you always assume your older brother knows everything and is basically right about everything.

I knew that Robbie was knocking around on the local rock club circuit – in the capitol city of Indianapolis, and the college towns of Bloomington, West Lafayette, and South Bend, the homes of, respectively, Indiana University (just 20 miles down the road from Nashville), Purdue University, and Notre Dame.

Of course, I wasn't old enough to get into bars or frat parties, so I never heard any of that. Just heard rumors of it, mostly. And that was farther than most local musicians ever got, so I was impressed, and I still expected that someday Robbie would "break through" and become a nationally-known star.

I grew up and moved away to pursue a career in journalism, but I always kept in touch with Brown County, and I knew a lot of the musicians of my era. My little brother became a rock'n'roll musician, so I more or less kept in touch with that whole scene, although I wasn't really around that much.

Some time in there, (the 70's, it turns out) I became aware of the "String Bean String Band", they were all the rage around these parts, although I wasn't around that much and didn't really move in their circles anyway (they were older and more hip – "the in crowd").

I heard String Bean String Band somehow got the nod to go out to the West Coast to make a record, and so, I assumed, Robbie's career plane was about to take off. Taxiing down the runway...

But some time later, probably a couple of years, I sort of got the word that that had not materialized. The String Bean plane never quite got off the ground, rock-star wise. Times were weird. Rock was giving way to Disco. The String-Beaners were rooted in folk and bluegrass, somehow both ahead of and behind the times at the same exact time.

More time passed, life went on apace. I would hear of Robbie's exploits here and there along with other music scene goings-on, but I never really saw him play out. I probably ran across him at parties or whatever, but I wasn't really clocking his career.

I knew that Robbie had married. I knew the woman he married through a mutual friend. But, once again, I wasn't really moving in those circles, socially. I'm actually a bit of a hermit, I guess.

Eventually, my parents got old and I moved back to Brown County and got a job on the local paper. And, serendipitously, though I was only there a few years, that time coincided with Robbie's next big career chapter – a series of recording projects with Slats Klug drawing upon the history and lore of Brown County, the place where we grew up.

Those records were exceptional and wonderful; a perfect marriage of folk legends and musical storytelling. This time, I had the chance to take in a lot more of the scene, see Robbie in action, and, once again, I was sure that this was his ticket to fame and fortune.

187

He is so much from and of Brown County; the very embodiment of what my generation felt about the place where we grew up.

They had a lot of success with those projects but, once again, the career plane never quite took off. The records never broke out to a national audience.

Some years passed. I lost my phony-baloney newspaper job. Then newspapers just started dying off. I was officially living in the past. Somehow, in spite of Pete Townshend's admonition, I did not die, but grew old. Older.

A few years later I heard that Robbie was in the local nursing home. I figured he was on his way out...

But then, a few years later, I would see him walking around town, and I would pick him up, maybe give him a ride to the drug store. He was walking with a cane, and was definitely looking like an old man. But then again, so was I.

But he was playing out around town and I would see him perform from time to time, at local wineries or bars.

You know, it's like the character says in that movie "Crossroads", "An old blues man is a good blues man." Musicians are like fine wine, they mellow and improve with age.

Old rock'n'rollers tell their stories... They have rambled far and wide, been in so many bands they can't remember them all, often end up with nothing but a song.

So, at some point fairly recently, Robbie mentioned to me that he had been looking for someone to help write his memoirs. I told him I would be glad to tackle the job.

I not only thought it was an interesting story that needed to be told, recorded, for Robbie's sake, and for Brown County's sake, I also thought it was a story that would probably resonate throughout the boomer generation.

It was probably the same in every little town in every rural county across the country – the local guitar hero who dreams of conquering the music world. (John Mellencamp grew up just down the road in Seymour.)

Like Paul Simon said in that song "Miracles and Wonder", "...every generation throws a hero up the pop charts..." Robbie is who the Brown County of my generation "threw up the pop charts".

Maybe he never made the cover of the Rolling Stone, but as he rightly points out, he's a local legend, having played a key role in the two most notable musical happenings in the Brown County of our generation, the "String Bean String Band", and the "Liar's Bench/My Brown County Home" series.

If you are not familiar with either of these projects, do yourself a favor and check it out. There's a String Bean Facebook page with a link to a Soundcloud account that has some of the String Bean material, and I'm told the main trove is at soundcloud.com/kypparila. Not sure about the Slats Klug/My Brown County Home CD's, but as of now I know you can buy them at Weedpatch Music in Nashville. I did and was reminded of just how great they are. What an amazing accomplishment!

So I have had the wonderful experience, over the past few months, of debriefing Robbie, helping him puke out all those stories, tales of a career, a life, the highs and lows.

One thing I learned as a newspaper reporter is, everybody has an interesting story to tell. People are interesting because of our common humanity and because of our individual uniqueness. Some combination of those two things make people's stories interesting to us. I'd much rather read biography than fiction because "Truth is stranger than fiction".

But this is not a biography, it is a memoir. If it were a biography, I would fact-check all this stuff, dates and names and places, try to interview everyone who is mentioned, you know, get their side of the story. I might press the subject for more details, the sinister specifics, etc.

That is not my intention. I'm just a ghost. I'm just here to help Robbie tell his story the way he always tells it. When I listened to him, this is what came out. Other than that, I make no claims or warranties.

As Bob Cheevers says: "It may not be true, but it happened to me."

I think it's an interesting story, whether you've been following Robbie's career – from afar or very near – for many years, your whole life, or whether you've never heard of him or Brown County or the 60's generation of Americans, or even rock'n'roll, I guess.

But who hasn't heard of rock'n'roll?

You may be wondering, now that we've come to the end of our ride together,

What's the moral of the story?

I guess it might be something like,

"The plane doesn't always take off."

"Big dreams, even good ones, don't always come true, even with perseverance, sacrifice and hard work."

"People's expectations are sometimes unrealistic, and our own limitations and liabilities may be obscured from us."

As John Lennon observed: "Life's what happens while we're busy making other plans..."

I've known a lot of good musicians, and I've heard a lot of people say, well, they never made it because they didn't have the guts to leave Brown County, go to L.A., go to New York City, where the real action is. If you want to make it, you have to get out of here.

I've never believed that. Just as many people went there, beat their brains out against the system, and "never made a nickel or a dime on the rock'n'roll thing", as Mojo Nixon said. Robbie had a pretty good run, but Bill Wilson got the short end of the stick, as far as I'm concerned.

It's all fate. It's all the luck of the draw. Being in the right place at the right time. A mystical combination of circumstances beyond our control or understanding. Some people make it, some people don't. Them's the breaks. You pays your money and you takes your chances...

Robbie went there. He paid his dues and he took his chances. He wasn't perfect, but he was good. He tried a lot of doors and scaled a lot of walls, one way and another. He finished the course set out for him.

He never made a million dollars. He's not famous, except maybe in Brown County, among a certain age group. Now, he's old, and, he's getting by OK, but he's not going to be making any more runs at the brass ring. He has a life, some friends, a warm, dry place to sleep and so forth.

I hope his story will be instructive, or at least entertaining.

Are you not entertained?

I hope you will come to appreciate Rob Bowden as much as I do.

I think you should, in Bob Dylan's turn of phrase, "write him letters and send him checks".

-Jeff Tryon, Spring, 2020

Made in the USA
Coppell, TX
23 December 2020

45103953R00115